TROUBLE FREE
CLEMATIS
THE
VITICELLAS

TROUBLE FREE
CLEMATIS

THE
VITICELLAS

JOHN HOWELLS

Photographs by the Author
Flower arrangements by Ola Howells
Consultant – Wim Snoeijer

GARDEN • ART • PRESS

British Library Cataloguing-in-Publication Data
A catalogue record for this book is available from
the British Library

Published by Garden Art Press,
a division of Antique Collectors' Club Ltd

FRONTISPIECE. *C.viticella* 'Blue Belle'.
ENDPAPERS. *C. viticella* 'Abundance' contrasts effectively with *robinia pseudoacacia* 'Frisia'.

Printed in England
by the Antique Collectors' Club Ltd., Woodbridge, Suffolk, UK
on Consort Royal Satin paper supplied by the Donside Paper Company,
Aberdeen, Scotland

List of Contents

Introduction

The Antique Collectors' Club

The Antique Collectors' Club was formed in 1966 and quickly grew to a five figure membership spread throughout the world. It publishes the only independently run monthly antiques magazine, *Antique Collecting*, which caters for those collectors who are interested in widening their knowledge of antiques, both by greater awareness of quality and by discussion of the factors which influence the price that is likely to be asked. The Antique Collectors' Club pioneered the provision of information on prices for collectors and the magazine still leads in the provision of detailed articles on a variety of subjects.

It was in response to the enormous demand for information on 'what to pay' that the price guide series was introduced in 1968 with the first edition of *The Price Guide to Antique Furniture* (completely revised 1978 and 1989), a book which broke new ground by illustrating the more common types of antique furniture, the sort that collectors could buy in shops and at auctions rather than the rare museum pieces which had previously been used (and still to a large extent are used) to make up the limited amount of illustrations in books published by commercial publishers. Many other price guides have followed, all copiously illustrated, and greatly appreciated by collectors for the valuable information they contain, quite apart from prices. The Price Guide Series heralded the publication of many standard works of reference on art and antiques. *The Dictionary of British Art* (now in six volumes), *The Pictorial Dictionary of British 19th Century Furniture Design*, *Oak Furniture* and *Early English Clocks* were followed by many deeply researched reference works such as *The Directory of Gold and Silversmiths*, providing new information. Many of these books are now accepted as the standard work of reference on their subject.

The Antique Collectors' Club has widened its list to include books on gardens and architecture. All the Club's publications are available through bookshops world wide and a full catalogue of all these titles is available free of charge from the addresses below.

Club membership, open to all collectors, costs little. Members receive free of charge *Antique Collecting*, the Club's magazine (published ten times a year), which contains well-illustrated articles dealing with the practical aspects of collecting not normally dealt with by magazines. Prices, features of value, investment potential, fakes and forgeries are all given prominence in the magazine.

Among other facilities available to members are private buying and selling facilities and the opportunity to meet other collectors at their local antique collectors' clubs. There are over eighty in Britain and more than a dozen overseas. Members may also buy the Club's publications at special pre-publication prices.

As its motto implies, the Club is an organisation designed to help collectors get the most out of their hobby: it is informal and friendly and gives enormous enjoyment to all concerned.

For Collectors — By Collectors — About Collecting

ANTIQUE COLLECTORS' CLUB
5 Church Street, Woodbridge Suffolk IP12 1DS, UK
Tel: 01394 385501 Fax: 01394 384434
——— or ———
Market Street Industrial Park, Wappingers' Falls, NY 12590, USA
Tel: 914 297 0003 Fax: 914 297 0068

Acknowledgements

Creating a book is a team effort and I have many to thank for their ready help. My publisher, Antique Collectors' Club, with staff members, Sandra Pond, Steve Farrow and Peter Robertson, produced this book as they did my other title, *The Rose and the Clematis as Good Companions*. Their admirable efforts were supplemented by the careful work of Michael Packard of Packard Publishing Ltd. Waiting in the wings were Susan Ryall and Brian Cotton who dealt with publicity, promotion and sales. The personal interest of Diana Steel enriched the effort at every stage.

I needed expert help with those viticellas with which I was less familiar and this assistance came from a number of willing sources – the late Uno Kivistik assisted with the Estonian, Wim Snoeijer with the Dutch, Brother Stefan Franczak with the Polish, Magnus Johnson and Bengt Sundström with the Swedish and Margareth Beskaravainaya with the Russian and Ukrainian viticellas. In the United Kingdom, Charles Chesshire introduced me to viticellas raised by Treasures of Tenbury, Harry Caddick to 'Jenny Caddick', Sheila Chapman to the very new 'Katheryn Chapman' and Robin Savill to his equally new 'Zingaro'.

Access to beautiful gardens has led me to the splendid garden of Burford House at Tenbury Wells, the ever expanding gardens of the Royal National Rose Society at St Albans, the model clematis garden of Mike Brown and the innovative garden of Beth Chatto. I have sharpened my photographic technique in the garden of my plantsman friend Lewis Hart. My knowledge of viticellas was enhanced by visits to Sweden, to the Botanic Garden and Hågelby Park in Stockholm, the garden of Magnus Johnson at Södertälje and the Uppsala Botanic Gardens. In Estonia I visited Erika Mahov's garden in Tallinin and the Kivistik family farm at Roogoja, in France the Bagatelle Gardens in Paris and in Holland the nursery of Jan van Zeost at Boskoop. Jerzy Bestjan gave invaluable biographical material about his friend Brother Stefan Franczak. For permission to reproduce the map on page 18 from *Slaktet Klematis* by Magnus Johnson, my thanks are due to Magnus Johnson and Bengt Sundström.

Of great advantage to me was my consultant Wim Snoeijer, eminent Dutch taxonomist and horticulturalist of Leiden University. On matters referred to him his opinion has been invaluable. Even with this help errors may have crept into the book – for these the author is entirely responsible.

My indefatigable literary assistant, Janet Hodge, has met my many demands with equanimity and efficiency. By my side has been my wife Ola, ever solicitous while providing practical help with her beautiful floral arrangements.

Introduction

The viticella clematis are undiscovered garden treasures. They are mostly overlooked because the 'Large Flowered' clematis are easier to display in garden centres. But the Large Flowered, though lovely, are flawed. Standing by are the just as lovely viticellas. These, almost as large, are more difficult to display because of their vigour. In the garden the viticellas make a larger show, are easier to grow, are hardy, and are trouble free. Why for instance grow a temperamental 'Lawsoniana' when it is surpassed for display by the abundance of the eye-catching velvety purple flowers of 'Etoile Violette' with its contrasting yellow stamens? The Large Flowered catch your eye in the garden centres; the viticellas catch your eye in the garden. The viticellas give such a big display that they could be termed 'the montanas of the summer'.

My discovery of the overwhelming value of the viticella clematis as a garden plant came from a garden experience. On one side of a long holly hedge grew forty viticella clematis. They had the difficult task of climbing on to a holly hedge, clambering to the other side of the holly and then falling down over a flint wall. They accomplished this and produced a striking, dazzling, display of multicoloured blooms. At the front of the same flint wall grew forty Large Flowered clematis. They struggled to make an impact despite infinite care in planting, in watering, in anti-fungal care, and in liquid fertilising. My gardening friends continually referred to the viticella display; in comparison the Large Flowered clematis were ignored. I had to conclude that the viticellas were clearly the better group for a trouble-free garden display.

PLATE 1. Viticella clematis in profusion.

PLATE 2. The delicate beauty of *C. viticella* 'Blekitny Aniol' (Blue Angel) blends well with rose 'Summer Wine'.

Clematis wilt, 'stem rot', is the flaw in the, otherwise lovely, Large Flowered clematis. It causes loss of young plants, which has to be countered by special techniques of planting, infinite care, and laborious anti-fungal measures. The problem of stem rot, does not arise with the viticellas. For some the Large Flowereds are worth the trouble but for most gardeners the viticellas are superior garden plants untouched by this disease. Growing more of the healthy viticellas is therefore a very good way of circumventing the problem while enjoying a group of clematis of great merit.

The range of features in the viticella flower is unsurpassed. Blooms can vary in size from tiny crosses to multi-petalled dinner plates that match the Large Flowered clematis in size. The plants climb from a few feet to 4.5m (15ft). The flowers often make nodding bells. Colours range from white through pink, red and blue to purple. In general the foliage is finely cut and attractive. Particularly, viticellas are easier for gardeners new to clematis to grow, as success is assured. Their appeal is international as they thrive well in average, cold or hot climates.

The viticellas, because of their diversity and vigour, are natural companions to shrubs and roses – an asset enhanced by the fact that they can be pruned almost to the ground in the autumn, thus allowing the host plant to revert to its naturalness for the winter. In severe climates it is easy to protect the crown and roots of the clematis.

The vigour of the viticellas makes them very popular in countries with low winter temperatures and where the growing period is short. In those climates any damage done to the stems in the winter will not matter as new growth appears from below soil level. The viticellas make rapid growth and flowers appear on the new growth made that summer. They also grow well in a Mediterranean-type climate; their home is the warm south of Europe.

Some viticellas have blooms that match the Early Large Flowered clematis in size, but the prominent feature of most of them is the abundance of blooms. What the smaller flowered ones lack in size they make up in a super-abundance of blooms which arrives in the first two years after planting. There is no period of waiting. The viticellas are so vigorous, so hardy, so reliable, so showy that they make garden plants second to none.

The book . . .
After an introductory discussion of the characteristics of the viticellas, this book will describe the small and medium bloomed viticellas before moving on to describe the Large Flowered ones. A supplementary list of scarcer plants will then be considered. A chapter on cultivation will show what easy plants they are to grow and this will lead to a chapter containing a full discussion of displaying viticella clematis. The book ends with a listing of the viticellas now lost to us.

PLATE 3.
C. viticella 'Alba Luxurians' at the Garden of the Rose, St Albans, UK.

CHAPTER ONE
The Viticella Group

The Clematis Genus

It may be useful to have a general idea of the features of the genus clematis to which the viticella group belongs (Figure 1).

The clematis are the only climbing members of the *Ranunculaceae* family which includes such flowers as the aconites, hellebores, anemones, buttercups, columbines, larkspurs and the tall delphiniums.

The genus clematis, as we shall see later, can be divided into twelve groups of which the viticellas are one. Of the twelve groups only one is herbaceous; the rest, including the viticellas, climb. Eleven groups are deciduous while the first group to flower in the flowering year is evergreen.

The clematis flower has one striking and unusual feature: it has no sepals which instead take on the function of the petals and are termed 'tepals'. Otherwise it conforms to a normal flower structure and in addition to the tepals, has male parts, stamens, and female parts, carpels. Clematis are classed as woody plants since the green soft stems soon become woody, adding to their hardiness. Clematis leaves are usually placed opposite each other on stems; in the Large Flowered groups there are usually three leaflets (ternate) and in the other groups they can take on many forms and be much divided.

Clematis has a long history and was described by such as Theophrastus (370-286 BC), Dioscorides (1st Century AD), Pliny the Elder (AD 23-79), and Galen (AD 129-199). When European herbals came to be written from the sixteenth century onwards the clematis were mentioned and described although their medicinal value was not great.

Most countries in the temperate regions of the Northern and Southern hemispheres have native clematis (Plate 4). There are over 300 wild clematis, more even than roses;

Table of the Family Ranunculaceae

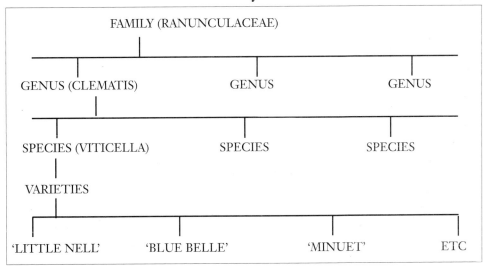

Figure 1. The place of the species viticella in the genus 'Clematis' in the family *Ranunculaceae*.

PLATE 4. Clematis *vitalba*, the rampant wild European clematis matches similar forms in many countries and together they girdle the world.

one of them, the viticella from southern Europe, is the main parent of the group considered in this book.

With cross-breeding within groups of clematis, and to a lesser extent between groups, new clematis appeared over time. Clematis enjoyed an enormous boost in its fortunes in the mid-nineteenth century when, due to the upsurge in plant hunting, the native species, especially the viticellas, were crossed with new large flowered clematis just come from China and Japan. The most successful cross was with *Clematis lanuginosa* from China. So large and lovely were the new large clematis that there was an enormous increase in production. Unfortunately, as we know today, *C. lanuginosa* was susceptible to clematis wilt (stem rot), and that weakness passed to the two groups of Large Flowered clematis, particularly the Early group. These two groups still suffer from that weakness today. The viticellas, however, do not have lanuginosa genes, and are free from clematis wilt.

Grouping Clematis for Garden Purposes

The gardener needs to know the general characteristics of the various groups of clematis so that he can take their special qualities into account when he plans his garden. The gardener also needs to know where the viticellas fit in the world of clematis.

At one time clematis were grouped or classified according to their pruning requirements. Though useful information, it told us nothing about the general characteristics of the clematis. Here I use a new, more useful, and easily understood classification (see Table 1).[1] Clematis are divided into twelve groups. The twelve are described here in the approximate sequence of flowering. The first starts blooming in early winter. The twelfth ends its blooming in late autumn.

PLATE 5. A mixture of three viticellas – 'Madame Grangé', 'Perle d'Azur', 'Abundance'.

TABLE 1
THE TWELVE CLEMATIS GROUPS

These groups are in the approximate order of flowering.

1.	The Evergreen group,	e.g. *C. armandii*
2.	The Alpina group,	e.g. *C. alpina* 'Frances Rivis'
3.	The Macropetala group,	e.g. *C. macropetala* 'Markham's Pink'
4.	The Montana group,	e.g. *C. montana* 'Mayleen'
5.	The Rockery group,	e.g. *C. x cartmanii* 'Joe'
6.	The Early Large-Flowered group	e.g. 'Nelly Moser'
7.	The Late Large-Flowered group	e.g. 'Jackmanii'
8.	The Herbaceous group,	e.g. *C. integrifolia* 'Rosea'
9.	The Viticella group,	e.g. *C. viticella* 'Madame Julia Correvon'
10.	The Texensis group,	e.g. *C. texensis* 'Gravetye Beauty'
11.	The Orientalis group,	e.g. 'Bill Mackenzie'
12.	The Late mixed group,	e.g. *C. flammula*

Group I   The first of the clematis to bloom are those of the **Evergreen** group. They flower from early winter onward. Examples would be *C. cirrhosa* and *C. armandii*, both making very large plants. They surprise everyone in winter with unexpected profuse flowering.

Group II   Then comes the hardy **Alpina** group. They make a selection of single multi-coloured bells from early spring on plants of medium height. Examples are 'Frances Rivis' and 'Jacqueline du Pré'.

Group III   Almost at once blooms the **Macropetala** group. Here we have not single but double nodding bells in a variety of colours from early spring onwards on plants of medium height. Examples are 'Markham's Pink' and 'Jan Lindmark'.

Group IV   Now comes the dramatic entrance of the **Montana** group. Indeed many, not aware of the beauties that have gone before, regard these as starting the clematis season. A plant can be huge, almost overpowering, and covered with thousands of blooms. Examples are 'Freda' and 'Mayleen'.

Group V   While the above have been catching attention, below them at almost ground level is the lovely **Rockery** group. Hardly exploited yet, this in time will be a popular section for the beauty of the delicate flowers. Examples are *C. marmoraria* and *C.* x *cartmanii* 'Joe'. They flower from early spring onwards.

Group VI   The **Early Large-Flowereds** bloom on growth made the previous year; so naturally they need little pruning or the blooms will be pruned away. They bloom from mid-spring onwards. Examples are 'Dr Ruppel', 'General Sikorski', 'Miss Bateman', 'Nelly Moser'.

Group VII   The **Late Large-Flowereds** bloom on growth made in the present season; so it makes sense to prune them severely in the early spring so as to encourage them to produce strong growth to make an abundance of flowers later. They bloom from early summer onwards. Examples are 'Comtesse de Bouchaud', 'Gipsy Queen', 'Hagley Hybrid' and 'Jackmanii'.

Group VIII   The **Herbaceous** group contains a number of wonderful plants for borders which clamber over other plants rather than climb. Being herbaceous they lose their stems in the winter. Examples are C. 'Durandii' and *C. integrifolia* 'Rosea'. They can flower from early summer onwards.

Group IX   The **Viticella** group is of outstanding merit and outclasses the Large Flowered group for garden worthiness. These clematis tend to send out very strong stems, sometimes to a great height, and are covered with a large number of medium-sized flowers from early summer onwards. They are trouble free, hardy, and have fascinating shapes and colours. Examples are 'Madame Julia Correvon' and 'Little Nell'. Their characteristics will be discussed in detail later.

Group X   The **Texensis** group of late summer again has distinctive qualities making bushes of medium height which tend to climb or clamber over other plants. The flowers are tulip or trumpet shapes of glowing colours. Each flower is of such beauty as to demand individual attention. Examples would be 'Gravetye Beauty' and 'Sir Trevor Lawrence'.

Group XI   The **Orientalis** group contains the truly yellow clematis. The yellows are vivid. Fine seedheads are a feature of this group. Bushes are usually of medium height but some can be tall. They flower mid-summer onwards but are more conspicuous in early autumn as colour disappears elsewhere in the garden. Examples are 'Bill Mackenzie' and *C. tangutica*.

Group XII   The **Late mixed group** brings the clematis year to an end in a burst of glory. Some of the plants are very vigorous as well as being scented and flower to late autumn. Examples are *Clematis flammula* and *Clematis potaninii*.

'Jacqueline du Pré'

'Bill Mackenzie'

armandii

'Mayleen'

'Joe'

'Durandii'

'Madame Julia Correvon'

PLATE 6.

We can see that we have two Large Flowered groups and ten Small Flowered groups. There are some general differences between the Large and Small Flowered. The large flowered clematis have lace-like roots, large flowers which are rarely scented and the plants can suffer from stem rot. Most, but not all of the small flowered clematis, on the other hand, have fibrous roots, have many small or medium sized flowers, are often scented, are easy to grow and rarely suffer from stem rot.

The range of clematis is probably much greater than the reader suspects. The twelve groups can be known easily by growing one clematis from each group – only twelve clematis in all. Reference will be made later to these groups as we look for trouble-free clematis to supplement the viticellas so as to give colourful blooms through the year.

Characteristics of the Viticella Clematis

The Name

Viticella simply means 'small vine'. We have to imagine that our distant forefathers were comparing our vine, large though it is, with the even larger grape vines.

The common name in English is 'Ladies Bower'. John Gerard (1545-1612) describes *Clematis viticella* in his *Herball* as he saw it in his garden on the 1st December 1597 and explains the name 'Ladies Bower' as follows: 'Which I take from his aptness in making Arbors, Bowers, and shadie couverturs in gardens.' The French Mathias de l'Obel (1538-1616), a contemporary of John Gerard, referred to it as *Clematis peregrina* (immigrant or foreigner), an apt description at the time for it came from southern Europe.

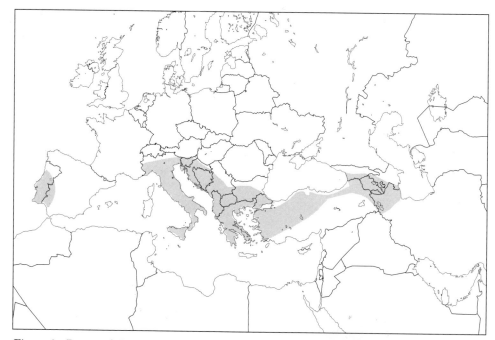

Figure 2. Range of *clematis viticella* in Europe and its neighbours. (M. Johnson)

Origin

The wild viticella grows in southern Europe in Mediterranean countries ranging from Portugal eastwards to Italy, Greece, Turkey, Iran and into western Asia (Figure 2). This wild clematis is the 'type' plant – that is the original plant of the species from which later cultivars were developed. Clematis were crossed with this wild clematis in a contrived way; crosses also occurred by chance. Again, new plants arose as 'chance seedlings'. These seedlings gave us the many cultivars that we have today. Use of *Clematis viticella* spread from southern Europe to middle and northern Europe; it was imported by Hugh Morgan to Britain in 1569.

Historical References

Plants were used for centuries for medicinal, domestic or commercial purposes. It was necessary to make a precise description of the named plant so that it could be recognised by the user. In Greek and Roman times physicians wrote their descriptions in manuscripts that were preserved. The most famous was Dioscorides of the 1st Century AD who described 600 plants and began descriptive botany.

For 1500 years European medicine was dominated by Greek and Roman medicine and early descriptions of plants were passed down to successive European physicians. Once printing was founded in the fifteenth century in Europe it was possible to produce books containing the description of plants and their medicinal use. As physicians from all countries studied in the great early French and Italian medical schools there was a common body of knowledge in Europe about plants and their medicinal uses. For instance, the well known English *Herball* of John Gerard was heavily indebted to other European Herbals, such as that of the Flemish herbalist Dodoens, and at the time of its writing was influenced by the French botanist de l'Obel, then in England, and by Carolus Clusius, the great French botanist then Professor of Botany at the Dutch University of Leiden.

As *Clematis viticella* was so easily available to Greek and Roman physicians it would be extraordinary if it did not feature in their works. Two clematis feature in the English Herbal of William Turner (1568) and one is probably *Clematis viticella*. *Clematis viticella* features in two forms in Gerard's *Herball* of 1597, not only because he had the plants in his botanic garden in Holborn, London, but because they were known to the European botanists/physicians contributing to his *Herball*. Gerard's viticellas were the type plant and a red form. 'This plant bringeth forth red floures'. In a later edition of the *Herball*, a third viticella was described – a double dark bluish-purple, *flore pleno* (double flower) – not to be confused with another double clematis hybridised in France much later in 1899, 'Purpurea Plena Elegans'.

Thereafter *C. viticella* featured in John Parkinson's (1567-1650) *Paradisus* of 1629, in Philip Miller's (1691-1771) *Dictionary* of 1724, in William Aiton's (1731-1793 *Hortus Kewensis* of 1789 and John Loudon's (1783-1843) *Arboretum et Fruticetum Britanicum* (Trees and Shrubs of Britain) 1835-1837.

Habit

The great characteristic of the viticella group is its vigour which, no doubt, comes from the type plant. John Gerard referred to it in his garden 'where they flourish exceedingly'. Three particularly vigorous viticellas are 'Polish Spirit' (page 59), 'Blue Belle' (page 39) and 'Södertälje' (page 63).

Figure 3. A double viticella, *Clematis viticella flore pleno*, illustrated in Johnson's Edition (1633) of Gerard's *Herball*.

PLATE 7. The wild *Clematis viticella* clambers over shrubs beside a pond in an English garden.

The viticella is classed as a semi-woody plant because, if not cut back to the ground each year, the stems become brown, strong and woody.

All the viticella clematis are deciduous, losing their leaves in winter. The viticellas climb or cling by the use of the petiole. John Gerard in his *Herball* of 1597 described it: 'it climeth aloft, and taketh hold with its crooked claspers upon every thing that standeth nere unto it!'. All the viticellas flower on new growth.

Height
Dwarf viticellas, such as *C. viticella* 'Nana', have been described. Most viticellas range from a height of 2.4m (8ft) to 4.5m (15ft); 6m (20ft) has been recorded. There is a tendency to climb higher in semi-shade.

Spread
Viticellas can spread from 2.4m (8ft) to 3.7m (12ft) dependent on the space and training given it by the gardener.

Colour range of flower
There are white, pink, red, blue and purple colours in the flowers. There are no yellows. With time colours tend to fade as they do in all clematis.

Some tepals have such a wide band of colour round the rim that the flower can almost be described, as bi-colour, for example in 'Minuet', 'Tango', 'Little Nell' and 'Walenburg'. (See Chapter 7, 'Table III', page 142)

Foliage
The stems are thin and twining giving support by using the petioles of the leaves. The leaves are long and consist of a variable number of leaflets which are often ovate in shape. There are usually three to seven leaflets of three segments (Plate 8). The leaflets are arranged in pinnate fashion. The leaves are invariably delicate and attractive. John Gerard in his *Herball* was to say 'it hath many leaves divided into devers parts'.

PLATE 8. A leaf, with seven leaflets, of *C. viticella* 'Abundance'.

PLATE 9. Vigorous *C. viticella* 'Blue Belle' climbs to the summit of a weeping pear tree (*Pyrus salicifolia* 'Pendula').

PLATE 10. Deep blue *C. viticella* 'Lady Betty Balfour' climbs to the top of a gazebo in autumn.

Fragrance

This is found in the type plant (according to John Gerard), in 'Betty Corning', and in *C.* 'Triternata Rubromarginata', where the scent comes from its other parent, *Clematis flammula*. Older writers refer to scent in *C. campaniflora*.

Seeds

These are not distinctive, have no attractive tail, but are usually viable and because of their ease of germination are much used in hybridising. Their qualities of vigour and disease resistance are valuable to their progeny. John Gerard in his *Herball* described them, 'the seeds be flat, plaine and sharp pointed!' (Plate 11).

Time of flowering

This is influenced by climate zone and altitude. In the Standard Zone, to be described later, this is from early summer until mid-autumn. An attraction of the viticellas is a three months or longer flowering period.

Number of flowers

The group is characterised by producing masses of bloom. Ernest Markham spoke of five thousand flowers on one plant. The large-flowered viticellas produce fewer blooms.

Hardiness

Rehder[2] suggests Zone IV, minimum temperature for *C. viticella* i.e. -20°C to -10°C, and for *C. campaniflora* Zone VI, -5°C to +5°C. Experience in Estonia suggests that the roots can be hardy at temperatures to -30°C. *C. viticella* has been grown in the Canadian prairie provinces of Saskatchewan and Manitoba where temperatures can fall below -40°C.

Roots

These are lace-like and were described by John Parkinson in his *Paradisus* in 1829 as follows: 'The roots are a bundle of brownish-yellow strong strings, running down deep into the ground' (Plate 12). Its strong roots encouraged gardeners to use it for grafting purposes.

Pruning

The flowers are produced on growth made in the year of flowering. Therefore the plant needs a severe pruning in the early spring so as to encourage new growth. As will be seen later, pruning is very easy in this group as it consists of simply cutting the stems to the ground.

Uses

The plants excel as companion plants and can be used in the garden for scrambling over heathers, roses, shrubs, trees or artificial supports. Some are suitable for growing in containers and others make excellent material for cutting. The fact that they make new growth from the ground each year makes it easy for the gardener to position the plant to his own requirements. This will be discussed in detail later.

PLATE 11. The short-tailed seeds of *C. viticella* 'Alba Luxurians'.

PLATE 12. The lace-like roots in a vicitella clematis.

Faults

These are very minor as is reflected by the great popularity of the plants once introduced to a gardener. Yet the seedheads are not attractive enough for decoration. Fragrance is lacking in most, but not all, viticellas. None is yellow coloured.

It would be pleasant to report that viticella clematis bloom throughout the year, but this is not so. They do bloom over a long period from early summer to mid autumn. It is possible, however, to extend the flowering period in three ways:
1. By using very late flowering types to extend the season into mid and late autumn, such as 'Polish Spirit' (page 59), 'Blue Belle' (page 39), 'Huldine' (page 48), 'Ville de Lyon' (page 67) and 'Lady Betty Balfour' (page 78).
2. By using the pruning techniques to be discussed later to produce a second crop of flowers.
3. By using trouble-free clematis from the other eleven groups to fill up the rest of the year. A separate chapter will be devoted to this.

Disease resistance

This is excellent. They do not suffer from clematis wilt (stem-rot). They are liable to suffer from 'mildew' in a wet season but this is easily corrected. Because of the disease resistance, and in addition their vigour, they are valuable for hybridising.

Soil requirements

Being fast growers Viticellas need nutrients. They also need ample water, good drainage so the roots can have oxygen, and light for growth. They tolerate a range of media from hot sun to a cold north wall.

The Life of the Viticella Flower

The viticella flower is a source of beauty to the gardener but its actual function, of course, is for reproduction. Colour and shade are there to attract and serve the insects that undertake the essential task of bringing the male and female parts of the plant together. The pollen must travel from the male anther, to the tip of the female carpel, the stigma, from where it travels to the ovary. A seed results which has the capacity to reproduce the plant (see Figure 5, page 27, the parts of the viticella flower). Below are described and illustrated the stages in the life of the viticella flower.

Stage I – Bud
No sepals.
No petals.
Tepals protect the bud interior.

Stage II – Opening Bud
Can now count the tepals.
Stamens in tight clump.
Colour of stamens comes from the anthers
and connective mainly.

Stage III – Early Flower
Tepals fully open.
Clump of stamens starting to open.
Stamens moving to lie flat against tepals.
Main colour of stamens still from anther.

Stage IV – Mature Flower
Tepals recurving.
Colour of tepals fading.
Stamens lie flat against tepals.
Colour of stamens now mainly from white
filaments.
Anthers changing colour to brown.

Stage V – Late Flower
Tepals are faded, damaged and falling away.
Stamens starting to fall off.
Carpels starting to protrude.

Stage VI – Early Stalk
Tepals gone.
Stamens falling off.
Carpels in centre protruding.

Stage VII – Late Stalk
Tepals and stamens gone.
Short carpel tails developing.

Stage VIII – Very Late Stalk
Some seeds developing from carpels.
Unfertilised carpels falling off.

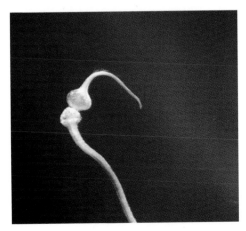

Stage IX – Seeds
Seeds alone on stalk.
All unfertilised carpels gone.

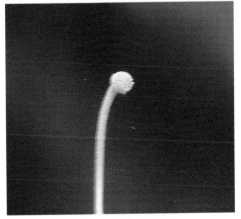

Stage X – Seeds Gone
Seeds ripened and gone.
Receptacle alone remains.
Will degenerate in time.
Flower has served its purpose and disappears.

The Structure of the Viticella Flower

Like all clematis the flowers of the viticellas have no sepals, these having taken over the function of petals and are called 'tepals'. There are four to seven tepals, more usually four. Exceptions are the double-flowered viticellas where four structures on the outside of the flower seem to take on the protective functions of sepals.

The plant is monoecious, having male and female parts in the same flower. The stamens, male parts of the flower, are usually well developed. In the female part of the flower there are a number of carpels where seeds are produced. The carpels are absent in the two double clematis 'Flore Pleno' and 'Purpurea Plena Elegans' and the stamens here take on the function of petals – petaloid stamens. Typically, the flowers are 4-6 cm (1½-2½in) across and are borne on stems of 7.5-10 cm (3-4in).

The flowers are usually on long stalks: either a solitary flower or in a cluster of three or more, characteristically a cyme of three. Frequently the blooms are single bells at first which may nod and open into saucer-shaped or flat flowers later. Some, however, are tubular in shape and two are doubles. The flowers often have unusual and attractive colouring and shape.

The cluster can be regarded as a cyme by some definitions of the term. The central flower in the cyme opens first (Figure 4). The length of the central stalk in relation to the other two is very variable. (The cluster behaves similarly in the late Large Flowered Group.)

Figure 4. Cyme of *C. viticella* 'Kermesina'.

PARTS OF FIGURE

LEAF

Leaflet –	part of a leaf
Petiole –	attaches leaf to stem. Viticellas uses this to cling.
Petiolule –	attaches leaflet to petiole
Bracts –	modified leaves growing near flower.

FLOWER

Tepals –	the petals of clematis
Flower bud –	
Peduncle –	a stalk bearing flowering cluster
Pedicel –	a stalk bearing one flower

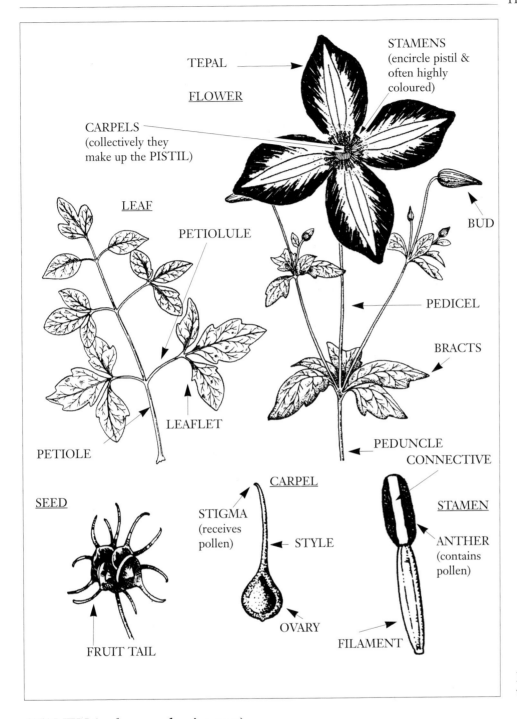

Figure 5. Diagram of a viticella flower.

STAMEN (male reproductive part)
Filament –   stalk of stamen
Anther –   contains pollen
Connective –   area between anthers

CARPEL (female reproductive organ)
Style –   stem of ovary
Stigma –   receives and nurtures pollen
Ovary –   produces seed
Fruit tails – showy tail to the seed. Not conspicuous in viticellas.
              (see also Plate 11, page 23)

Defining What Is A Viticella

Moore and Jackman in their book *The Clematis as a Garden Flower* (1877) give definitions of the various groups of clematis and defined the Jackmanii and the Viticella Groups as follows:

The JACKMANII GROUP – 'summer and autumn bloomers, flowering successively in profuse continuous masses on summer shoots; woody climbers.'

The VITICELLA GROUP – 'summer and autumn bloomers, flowering successively in profuse masses on summer shoots; woody climbers.'

The only difference in the two groups is that Moore and Jackman used the word 'continuous' when referring to the Jackmanii group. However A.G. Jackman in the *Gardener's Chronicle* of 8th March 1890 writes: 'The viticella and Jackmanii types flower at the same time in profuse continuous masses on the young summer shoots till frosts come, making them very attractive.' We now find the term 'continuous' is

PLATE 13. *Clematis* 'Venosa Violacea' of the Viticella Group.

PLATE 14. *Clematis* 'Victoria' of the Jackmanii Group.

used for both groups, making no difference in the definition of the two.

Dr Jules Le Bele[4] in 1898 talks of two types of Viticella, Ordinary and Large flowered (Jackmanii). The first type consists of *clematis viticella* and a number of hybrids. All are characterised by racemes of cross-shaped medium-sized flowers. They flower later than the second type. The second type has larger flowers than the first and is characterised by tufts of flowers in the form of cymes; this group flowers earlier than the 'ordinary' group.

Le Bele's definition is not over-helpful. By today's definition racemes of flowers are not characteristic of the 'ordinary' viticella group. The cyme is more characteristic. However the cyme is the same in both the 'ordinary' viticella group and the Jackmanii group, characterised in both by the central flower opening first and the variable length of the central stalk in relation to the other stalks. Furthermore in the second group Le Bele includes clematis listed, by others as belonging to Group 1, – 'Mme Grangé', 'Mme Furtada-Heine', 'Magnifica', 'Etoile Violette'.

Magnus Johnson, eminent clematarian and taxonomist, refers to the viticella group as 'Cultivars near related to the species *C. viticella*'. For Johnson it would appear that it is the amount of the wild viticella involved in the pedigree that counts. Ernest Markham in his book *Clematis* in 1935 refers to it as 'a variable species'. Christopher Lloyd in his *Clematis* of 1989 states '*C. viticella* has a place in the parentage of so many hybrids that I am reluctant to use its title for a group that is bound to be arbitrary'. Lloyd agrees with Markham about the looseness of definition.

Wim Snoeijer in his *Checklist of Clematis*, 1996, refers to the two groups as follows:

Clematis Jackmanii Group
Description: Woody climbers flowering on old wood in spring and/or on young shoots in summer and early autumn. Leaves pinnate with simple leaflets, rarely ternate or simple leaves. Flowers upright to horizontal or semi-nodding, spreading to semi-campanulate, 6-15cm across. Tepals 4 to 6, usually obovate in shape, white, red-purple, blue, violet-blue or purple-violet. Fruitstyle plumose. Derived originally from *Clematis viticella* crossed with plants belonging to the Patens Group. New introductions are getting closer to the Patens Group but maintenance of the Jackmanii Group is still worthwhile.

Clematis Viticella Group
Description: Woody climbers flowering on young shoots in summer and early autumn. Leaves pinnate with simple, ternate or pinnate leaflets. Flowers horizontal to nodding, campanulate to spreading, 3-12cm across. Tepals 4 to 6, rather thin, obovate in shape, white, red-purple, blue, violet-blue or purple-violet. Fruitstyle sparesely plumose to glabrous. Usually chance seedlings of *Clematis viticella*. Many are not straight cultivars anymore because of interbreeding with plants belonging to other cultivar-groups

From the above descriptions, it can be seen that the two Groups show many likenesses. There few differences and these are minor. To separate the Groups is not easy; the viticellas are more likely to be campanulate and nodding, to have less feathery fruit styles, to have smaller flowers, and not to suffer from stem-rot (wilt).

It has to be concluded that there is no clear-cut differentiation between the Viticella and Jackmanii Groups. In selection here, plants are included in the viticella group if they have a strong component of viticella in their pedigree, flower on young wood, flower from mid-summer onwards, are vigorous, tend to bell-shaped flowers, and are disease resistant. In such a variable group there is bound to be room for differing opinions on grouping. In the last analysis the gardener wants a trouble-free group.

Pronunciation

It is more important to be understood than to abide by the finer points of pronunciation.

Clematis

In classical Greek our plant was named by, for example, Dioscorides, as 'clematitis' (connected to clematis) or 'clematides' (resembling clematis). 'Clematis' was reserved for the periwinkle (Vinca). Dioscorides also used the term *Clematis altera* for the clematis that were not periwinkles (*altera* – 'the other'). *Clematis viticella* was known to the Greeks and the Romans, being native to their countries. The four blue tepals of the viticella would invite comparison with periwinkle. At some point in the late medieval period the name left the periwinkle and firmly stood for our climber.

As all the authorities are agreed, there is no difficulty with this name. We can consider it under three syllables:

cle	has a short 'ĕ' and the syllable is pronounced
KLE	as in 'clĕric'
ma-	'a' is a short 'ă' as in 'ăpart'
'tis	'i' is short and 'tis' rhymes with 'hiss'

For clematis we have: klĕ   mă   tĭs

Plural is clematises but its awkwardness has led to its being discarded. Therefore 'clematis' is used for one or more than one plant.

Viticella

We can consider this word under three syllables and if we follow W. T. Stearn[3] we find its pronunciation is straightforward as follows:

vit	has a long 'ī' and thus becomes 'veet' and not 'i' as in ice
-i-	is a long 'ī' and therefore 'ee'
'cella	has a 'c' before 'e' and syllable therefore has 'c' pronounced like an 'S' as in 'centre' ie 'sentre', 'ă' is a hard 'a' as in Africa Thus 'cella' becomes 'sella'

For 'viticella' we therefore have: Veet-ee-sella The plural of viticella is viticellas.

Footnotes
1. Howells, J. (1992) A Gardener's Classification of Clematis. *The Clematis*. p.34.
2. Rehder, A. (1900) *Manual of Cultivated Trees and Shrubs*. Dioscorides Press, Portland, Oregon.
3. Stern, W.T. (1992) *Botanical Latin*. David & Charles, Newton Abbot.
4. Le Bele, Jules (1898) *The Garden*. 24 September p.240.

PLATE 15. *C. viticella* 'Madame Julia Correvon' harmonises with climbing rose 'Super Star'.

PLATE 16. *C. viticella* 'Margaret Hunt' on the left and *C. viticella* 'Margot Koster' on the right.

CHAPTER TWO
Small and Medium Flowered

In this chapter thirty-four garden-worthy viticellas are introduced and presented in alphabetical order. The type plant, *Clematis viticella*, is taken first. In each case the first name of the plant is that given and used in the country of origin.

First, in each case there is a general description of the plant and its merits. Second, technical data given for each plant together with any Award of Garden Merit (AGM) of the Royal Horticultural Society of the United Kingdom. Third, consideration of a viticella may stimulate points of interest – intriguing facts, episodes, connections or historical links. A submission is made for each flower.

CLEMATIS VITICELLA

This is the 'type' plant of the group, the original plant from the wild that has its genes in all the members of the group. It grows wild in southern Europe and western Asia and produces beautiful deep blue, dancing, bell-shaped flowers in profusion. A garden-worthy plant. Has some fragrance as well. Excellent when grown on an arbour, as the old gardeners knew.

Name Meaning 'a little vine'. Common names: 'Purple Virgin's Bower'; 'Ladies Bower'; 'Vine Bower Clematis'.

Origin From southern Europe and western Asia. Introduced to England in 1569 by Hugh Morgan.

Habit Climber. Vigorous. Height to 3.6 m (12 ft). Prolific flowerer.

Flowers Nodding campanulate or saucer-shaped when fully open; 4-6cm (1½-2½in) across; 4-6 tepals of deep violet or purple or rosy purple colour; colour lighter in centre and at base of tepals; back of tepal is lighter in colour with deeper bar at centre; tepals are obtuse in shape and recurve at ends; anther – yellow; filament - greeny white. Pistil – greeny white; flowers on long stalks 5-10cm (2-4in) either single or in groups; seed heads have short inconspicuous tails; fragrant.

Foliage As described for group. Mid-green.

Special Features Because of its vigour and disease resistance used extensively for hybridising.

Accurate in 1597

The old writers may not have had that extra knowledge we call 'scientific' but their descriptive powers lacked nothing. They had to be accurate for they needed the right plant for their maladies. John Gerard had ten clematis in his garden at Holborn, London, including *Clematis viticella*. In his *Herball* of 1597 he describes it as follows ('peregrina' stood for 'foreign'):

'That which L'Obel describeth by the name of Clematis peregrina, hath very long and slender stalks like the Vine, which are joynted, of a darke colour; it climeth aloft, and taketh hold with his crooked claspers upon every thing that standeth nere unto it; it hath many leaves divided into divers parts; among which come the floures that hang upon slender footstalkes, something like to those of Pervinkle, consisting onely of foure leaves, of a blew colour, and sometimes purple, with certaine threds in the middle; the seeds be flat, plaine and sharpe pointed. The roots are slender and spreading all about'.

'ABUNDANCE'

This plant is well named as its blooming is prolific on a plant that can grow to 6m (20ft). A classic trouble-free vigorous viticella coming into the red section of the group, with blooms that are attractively textured. Highly recommended.

Name Signifies abundant blooming.

Origin Hybridised by Francisque Morel in France about 1900. Seedling passed to William Robinson and Ernest Markham at Gravetye Manor, Sussex, UK and on to Jackmans of Woking, Surrey, UK, after Ernest Markham died in 1947. Jackman of Woking introduced it.

Habit Deciduous. Climber. Vigorous. Grows to 6m (20ft). Prolific flowerer. Flowers mid-summer to early autumn. Grows at any aspect.

Flower Semi-nodding at first; opens to saucer shape; up to 9cm (3½in) across; 4-6 tepals coloured pinky mauve and wavy edged; tepals may recurve at tips and are textured; central white bar at back of tepal; creamy-green anther and white filament; light green prominent carpels; long flower stalks.

Foliage Mid-green. 5-7 leaflets. Conforms to group.

The Redoubtable William Robinson

Gravetye Manor in Sussex, England, became the focus of clematis growing in England when it passed, in 1884, into the hands of William Robinson. Although from humble origins in Ireland, Robinson became a wealthy man through his writing and, aged sixty-four, could afford to buy this large estate. His passionate views on garden planning broke down the rigid patterns of the past and introduced the informality we know today.

His interest in clematis produced a book *The Virgin's Bower* in 1912. He admired the viticella which he thought 'has given us some of the best garden clematis'. He advocated sowing the viticella seed in hedgerows; a truly wonderful notion. He died in 1935, aged ninety-seven, and his friend and head gardener, Ernest Markham, carried on his work with clematis.

'ALBA LUXURIANS'

This plant has one of the most eye-catching and intriguing flowers in the garden. Clematis have no sepals and it is as if here green sepals are demanding a share of the flower. The result is attractive and dramatic. In addition, the plant is vigorous and reliable. It flowers for a long time, right into the autumn.

Name Signifies white and luxuriant.

Origin Raised by Veitch at their Coombe Wood Nursery, Langley, Slough, UK and introduced in 1900.

Habit Deciduous. Climber. Vigorous. Grows to 5m (16ft). Prolific flowerer. Flowers mid-summer to mid-autumn.

Flower May be semi-nodding at first and soon opens flat; flower up to 8cm (3in) across; 4-5 tepals; tepals are white or pale violet in colour with violet especially towards the edges; tepals may have areas of bright green especially in early flowers where there may be more green than white; tepals may twist at tips and edges; margins are wavy; at back of tepal there is a greeny-white central bar; anthers are dark purple with greeny-white filaments; carpels are light brown; flower on long stalks.

Foliage Mid-green. 5-7 leaflets with three lobes.

Special Features Award of Garden Merit 1931. 'Caerulea Luxurians' is a seedling of 'Alba Luxurians' which has no green and is white rinsed in blue.

The House of Veitch

The Veitch family, the raisers of 'Alba Luxurians', was one of the most successful of nursery owners. The firm's story begins with John Veitch (1752-1839) who started the business in Exeter, UK, in 1832. The business was developed by his son, James Veitch (1792-1863), who also opened a branch in Chelsea, London. The London branch passed to his son James Veitch (1815-1869) who opened branch nurseries, including one at Coombe Wood, Slough, where 'Alba Luxurians' was raised. After James' death the business passed to (Sir) Harry James Veitch who brought the firm to its high point, only for it to decline and to close down in 1914. The Veitch dynasty sponsored plant hunters; the most notable was E.H. Wilson who brought thirteen clematis, including *C. armandii*, *C. veitchiana* and *C. montana* 'Rubens', back to England.

'BETTY CORNING'

A subdued beauty, this is a viticella with a number of virtues. The flowers have a most attractive bell shape. It is the first major American clematis to be bred. It has fragrance - one of only three viticellas. The delicate bells come in profusion, dancing in the breeze. The flowers may be delicate but the plant is vigorous.

Name After American lady horticulturist.

Origin Raised by Mrs Betty Corning in 1933 from a seedling given her. Introduced by the firm of Steffens in the USA. Assumed to be a cross of the native American *C. crispa* and a *C. viticella*.

Habit Deciduous. Climber. Vigorous. Grows to 3m (10ft). Flowers from early summer to mid autumn.

Flower Nodding bell-shaped flower with recurving tips; flower up to 7cm (2½in) across; 4 tepals coloured pale violet with deeper violet at edge; colours fade; serrated edges to tepals; back of tepals are paler with three distinct ridges; anthers are green with yellow filaments; the prominent carpels are green; flowers on long stalks; flower is fragrant.

Foliage Usually five leaflets with three lobes.

Special Features Suitable for container culture and for cutting. Can be compared with other bell-shaped viticellas as 'Pagoda', 'Elvan', 'Blue Boy', 'Hendersonii', 'Etoile Rose', 'Sturminster' and *Clematis viticella*.

Clematis From Potatoes

Mrs Elizabeth Corning II was the twenty-year old bride of Erastus Corning, a distinguished citizen and Mayor of Albany, New York State. She moved to Corning Hill after her wedding and there, over time, she created a fine garden. She was a former President of the Garden Club of America and was on the board of innumerable botanic gardens.

Mrs Corning discovered what we now call *C. viticella* 'Betty Corning' when out walking one day in 1932 in Bertha Street, Albany. The daughter of a clematarian she was ever watchful to spot clematis. Luck came to her that day for she spied an unknown beautiful clematis in a garden. The gardener could give it no history having been given it by a friend. He brought the cutting home in a potato, its rooting medium. Betty Corning was given a large piece of stem which she successfully propagated. A plant went to Steffen's nursery which introduced it, giving it her name.

'BLEKITNY ANIOL' (BLUE ANGEL)

Light blue clematis are rare. The colouring of this Polish plant makes a great appeal, though more violet than blue to close inspection. The wavy margins and ruffled surface make for an unusual and appealing flower. A plant for every aspect, it is vigorous and reliable.

Name Polish for 'Blue Angel'.

Origin Bred by Brother Stefan Franczak in Warsaw, Poland, and introduced in 1990.

Habit Deciduous. Climber. Grows to 4m (13ft). Profuse flowerer in continuous crops from early summer to early autumn. Grows in any aspect.

Flower Semi-nodding at first, it soon opens flat and is up to 11cm (4in) across; 4-6 tepals that overlap at base; colour of tepals pale violet, darker at edge and white at base, strongly fading; pronounced ruffled surface; very wavy edges; at back of tepal an attractive central deep violet bar; anthers are pale yellow with white filaments; the prominent carpels are off-white.

Foliage Five leaflets, either three lobed or solitary. Mid-green.

Special Features 'Blekitny Aniol' has the colouring of 'Prince Charles' and 'Perle d'Azur' but is a paler violet than both. Paler also than 'Emilia Plater'. Suitable for a container and for cutting.

A Jesuit Brother and Clematis

The Roman Catholic Church is widespread and its missions are found everywhere. These missions have sometimes been the home of famous plant hunters. Père Armand David (1826-1900) comes to mind. *C. armandii* and the *C. heracleifolia* var. *davidiana* were named after him. Père Jean Delavay (1834-1895) introduced a massive collection of plants to Europe from China, including *Clematis chrysocoma*.

A church brother contributes in another way today. Brother Stefan Franczak is one of the world's most successful clematis hybridists and he gave 'Blekitny Aniol' and 'Emilia Plater' to the world. One of fourteen children, Stefan was born at Jeziorna, Poland in 1917. After training in agriculture and horticulture he joined the Jesuits in 1948 and two years later moved to the Jesuit House of Writers in Warsaw as Keeper of the Monastery Garden. His life's work there has given us over twenty new clematis. More than this, for his other great love, the day lily (*Hemerocallis*), he introduced eighty-four new varieties!

'BLUE BELLE'

If you want a vigorous plant in the garden, then this is it. Perhaps 'blue' is a misnomer for 'purple' is more exact. But the 'Belle' is true enough. One of the tallest viticellas it still has comparatively large blooms which are eye-catching because of the light centre against a very deep purple. Flowers rather later than most viticellas and useful as an autumn flowering plant.

Name Designates plant as a blue beauty.

Origin Raised in 1925 by Ernest Markham at Gravetye Manor, Sussex, UK.

Habit Deciduous. Climber. Very vigorous. Grows to 6m (20ft). Profusion of flowers. Flowers late summer to mid-autumn. Suitable for all aspects.

Flower Open flower to 11cm (4in); 6 tepals with no overlap; colour of tepals is very dark purple with slightly darker central band; serrated edges, light mauve back; prominent stamens with yellow anthers and white filaments; carpels are off-white; flowers on long stems.

Foliage 5 leaflets either solitary or 2-3 lobes.

Special Features Suitable for cutting. Received Award of Merit by Royal Horticultural Society of UK in 1935.

Ernest Markham of Gravetye Manor

After a successful career in horticultural writing the bachelor William Robinson bought Gravetye Manor in Sussex, UK, and Ernest Markham became his friend and head gardener. Ernest Markham not only hybridised many clematis, including viticellas, but was also given a large number of seedlings by the great French hybridist Francisque Morel. He was busy hybridising viticellas in World War II but died in 1947; these viticellas were lost. His book *Clematis* was published in 1935; he was enterprising enough to include a chapter on American clematis by the famous American clematarian, J.E. Spingarn.

'BLUE BOY'

Viticellas can be so tall. This Canadian plant is one of the exceptions growing only to 2.5m (8ft). It is not a strong climber and is therefore an ideal clamberer over a shrub or support. Flowers are dancing bells produced continuously over a long period and easily seen as the plant grows near the ground.

Name Designates colour of plant.

Origin Raised by Dr F.L. Skinner at Dropmore, Manitoba, Canada, in 1947. Became known after raiser wrote about plant in 1966 in his book *Horticultural Horizons*. Introduced to commercial market recently. Same parents as *C.* 'Hendersonii' (*C. viticella* x *C. integrifolia*).

Habit Deciduous. Semi-shrub. Vigorous. Grows to 2.5m (8ft). Strong growth at top. Profuse flowering. Very hardy. Flowers continuously mid-summer to early autumn.

Flower Nodding bell-shape up to 8cm (3½in) across; 4 tepals with recurving tips; tepal is deep violet inside with ruffled surface and at centre rosy tinge to the violet; on back colour is violet with a lavender deeply ridged bar; anther yellow with white filaments; carpels greeny white; flowers on long stalks.

Foliage 7 leaflets. Mid-green. Leaflets entire or 3-lobed.

Special Features Differentiate from 'Hendersonii' (later) and 'Eriostemon' (see Supplementary List, page 92).

Beauty from the cold north

Dr F.L. Skinner, the raiser of 'Blue Boy' and distinguished horticulturalist, was thwarted from growing the Large Flowered clematis in the harsh winter climate of Manitoba, Canada. They just did not survive. He turned his attention to the other groups with great benefit to us. His interest was to produce hardy plants. Well-known Skinner plants include the macropetalas, 'White Swan' (1961), 'Blue Bird' (1962), 'Rosy O'Grady' (1964). Another is 'Western Virgin' ('Prairie Traveller's Joy') (1962), which makes a massive plant up to 10m (35ft) covered with bloom in the autumn. An immigrant Scot, his great contribution to horticulture earned him an honorary doctorate of the University of Manitoba.

CLEMATIS CAMPANIFLORA

Opinions are mixed about this large plant. Some argue that it takes up too much space for the colour it gives. Others argue it is a misuse of the plant to grow it alone. Let it scramble over dark shrubs and trees and so show off its myriads of small delicate bell-shaped blooms. It is very reliable and vigorous. It also flowers into the autumn.

Name Meaning - campanulate (bell-shaped) flower. Common names - 'Hairbell Virgin's Bower', 'Bell flowered Virgin's Bower'.

Origin Plant native to Portugal and Spain. Use spread to rest of Europe and arrived in England in 1810. Said to have been discovered by a Professor F.A. Brotero on the hedges of the road from Coimbra to Oporto and described by him in 1804.

Habit Deciduous. Climber. Very vigorous up to 6m (20ft). Profusion of very small blooms. Flowers mid-summer to mid-autumn. Any aspect. Comes true from seed.

Flower Nodding bell-shaped; 3cm (¼in) across; 4 tepals; tepals inside are white or pale violet with more pronounced violet at edges; tips recurve; tepals on back are white tinged with violet, deeper at base; tepals said to get bluer as they age; anthers are yellow fading to brown; filament greeny-white; green connective; prominent pistil is off-white; flowers solitary or in cymes; early writers refer to fragrance; stalks 3-7cm (1-2½in).

Foliage 5-7 leaflets up to 15cm (6in) long. Entire or lobed. Finely cut. Dark green.

Special Features There is a cultivar 'Lisboa', raised in the Lisbon Botanical Garden in 1956, that has more violet colour and larger bloom. A cross of *C. campaniflora* with *C. viticella*.

Mr Mulligan and 'Campaniflora'

Opinions can vary greatly over a particular plant. 'Campaniflora' demonstrates this. Richard Gorer in his book *Climbing Plants* dismisses it with 'it is not sufficiently showy to be given a prominent place'. Ernest Markham finds the plant 'graceful', the flower 'charming', and so many flowers that it produces 'a large lace-like curtain of soft blue'.

Mr Mulligan of Wisley, writing in the *Garden Chronicle* in 1936 is the real admirer: 'exceedingly graceful', 'a loose lacy curtain of quiet beauty', 'revels luxuriantly', 'a perfect shower of blooms'. Mr Mulligan must have it.

'ELVAN'

There is something 'old world' about this plant covered with lovely purple and white nodding bells. The more you live with it the more you like it. It climbs well on other plants but care needs to be taken to have a colour background that shows off its intrinsic beauty.

Name Not sure what link Barry Fretwell sees between this delicate beauty and blue fine-grained granite. I would like 'elven' ('impish dwarf').

Origin Raised by Barry Fretwell of Peveril Nursery, Devon, UK, and introduced in 1979.

Habit Deciduous climber. Vigorous to 3.5m (12ft). Profusion of flowers from mid-summer to early autumn. Any aspect.

Flower Nodding bell-shaped and 5cm (2in) across bell; 4 tepals, the tips of which may recurve and twist; tepals are dark purple on the inside, patterned and have central white bar; wavy edges; back of tepals are dark purple with deeper central bar; anther yellow-green; filament green; pistil off-white and protuberant.

Foliage Light green. 5-7 leaflets - entire.

Special Features Compare with 'Pagoda', 'Betty Corning', 'Sturminster' and *C. viticella*.

The Bell-Shaped Flower in the Viticellas

The lightest coloured, white, and the smallest is *C. campaniflora*. Cannot be missed as the plant is so large and the flower so small. Then comes a group of three with mixed white and purple flowering, 'Pagoda', 'Elvan' and 'Betty Corning', in order of size of bloom. All continuous blooming and enchanting. Then come two blues, 'Hendersonii' and 'Blue Boy', the former being the deeper and the latter the lighter blue. Both are long flowering. Lastly comes 'Etoile Rose' – large drooping trumpets cover this gorgeous plant. It has a brilliant rosy colouring. All are lovely but everyone has to have 'Etoile Rose' (page 44).

'EMILIA PLATER'

This new viticella from Poland, once more widely known, is likely to become very popular. The combination of a crêpey surface and wavy margins make it a most attractive flower. The colour, a pure violet-blue, also gives it appeal. Showy in a container, with yellow flowers and over dark foliage.

Name After a Polish heroine.

Origin Raised by Brother Stefan Franczak of Warsaw, Poland, between 1988-1990.

Habit Deciduous climber. Vigorous. Prolific bloomer. Grows to 3.5m (12ft). Any aspect except north. Flowers mid-summer to mid-autumn.

Flower Slightly nodding at first, it opens to a flat flower of 10cm (4in) diameter; 4 tepals that are of violet-blue colour with deeper violet bar at centre; they have crêpey surface and wavy edges; back of tepal is pale violet with prominent purple bar at centre; anthers are yellow and connective is green; filament white; pistil is greeny-white.

Foliage Mid-green. 5-7 leaflets - usually entire.

Special Features Compare with 'Prince Charles', 'Blekitny Aniol' and 'Perle d'Azur', all of which have paler violet colours. A plant for a container.

The Flowers with a Ruffled Surface

Originally we had 'Perle d'Azur'. Then came 'Prince Charles', to be followed by 'Blekitny Aniol' and now there is 'Emilia Plater'. 'Kasmu' (*Syn.* 'Signe') from Estonia will soon be on the international stage. All four also have the merit of having various shades of light violet; this light shade appeals as it is uncommon in clematis. 'Perle d'Azur' has the largest flower and the least ruffled surface. 'Emilia Plater' is of the deepest violet and 'Blekitny Aniol' of the lightest, but very ruffled 'Kasmu' may prove to be an ever deeper violet (Plate 37, page 83).

'ETOILE ROSE'

This is one of the finest of all clematis. It gives a generous production of eye-catching trumpets in glowing colours for three months. Greatly sought after. As the trumpets droop, encourage plant to grow to full height so that trumpets can be seen from below. It has a small weakness, susceptibility to mildew, that should deter no one. Prevent this defacing your gorgeous blooms by giving weekly doses of fungicide into the ground around plant starting before buds appear.

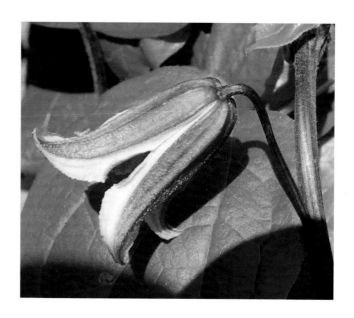

Name Meaning - rosy star.

Origin Raised in France by V. Lemoine et Fils and introduced in their catalogue list No. 158 in 1903. The plant resulted from a cross between *C.* x *globulosa* and an unknown viticella. *C.* x *globulosa*, described first in 1897, was a cross between *C. douglassi* var. 'scottii' and *C. coccinea* (*C. texensis*). Mr Mark Fenwick of Abbotswood, Stow-on-the-Wold, obtained a plant from France about 1930. It was grown there for many years and had an Award of Merit in 1959 from the Royal Horticultural Society, England. This plant was probably the precursor of subsequent English plants.

Habit Deciduous. Climber or semi-shrub. Vigorous. Prolific flowerer. Grows to 4.5m (15ft). Flowers mid-summer to early autumn. Likes sunny aspect. Liable to attacks of mildew.

Flower Nodding trumpet-shaped flower; 4 textured tepals up to 5cm (2in) long, recurving at tips; diameter of flower is 5cm (2in); outside of tepal has a deep violet-pink stripe in centre and violet pink near edges; inside of tepal has central broad rosy-pink band; near tip the bar narrows and replaced by pinky-white strip; anther pale greeny-yellow turning brown; filament white; pistil is off-white; long firm stalks.

Foliage 7-9 leaflets, either single entire or 3-

When Is A Viticella Not A Viticella?

Opinions cannot always agree of course and debate adds interest. 'Etoile Rose' and 'Pagoda' are members of the Texensis Group or are they viticellas? A strong case can be made for both being viticellas. The parentage given for 'Etoile Rose' shows that *C. texensis* made up only 25% of its make-up. It was bred by Lemoine et Fils in France, and not Jackmans of the UK, which was responsible for the group of nineteenth century texensis plants, the so-called 'Wokingensis Hybrids'. Like 'Pagoda', the trumpets of 'Etoile Rose' point downwards; this is a characteristic of viticellas and not the Texensis Group. The foliage of both 'Pagoda' and 'Etoile Rose' is that of the Viticella Group.

'ETOILE VIOLETTE'

This is one of the most popular of all clematis. Preferred by some to 'Jackmanii' as it gives a very large display of velvety dark purple blooms with light centres. Very reliable. Bear its colour in mind and display against a light background or into a light rose such as the rose 'New Dawn'.

Name Meaning - violet star.

Origin Raised by M. Francisque Morel of Lyon-Vaise, France and introduced in 1885.

Habit Deciduous climber. Very vigorous. Height to 3.5m (12ft). Profuse flowerer. Hardy. Flowers early summer to early autumn. Any aspect.

Flower Horizontal flower up to 12cm (4¼in); 4-6 tepals do not overlap; dark purple velvety tepals; serrated edges; on back lighter purple; anther greeny-yellow; filaments white; pistil off-white.

Foliage 5 leaflets of 3 lobes.

Special Features Award of Garden Merit. Royal Horticultural Society, UK, 1984.

The Great Morel

Francisque Morel (1849-1925), the raiser of 'Etoile Violette', was arguably the greatest hybridist of clematis ever. The Jackman Nursery of Woking, UK, produced more clematis, but Morel was innovative. He realised that the Large Flowered clematis were doomed; all Europe was attacked by stem rot (wilt). He set about finding a solution. The knowledge we have today was unavailable to him but by

practical experience he had learned that viticellas resisted stem rot. So he set about hybridising the viticellas 'Madame Julia Correvon', 'Royal Velours', 'Etoile Violette'. His great breakthrough came with 'Ville de Lyon' which he claimed was free of wilt with a flower of a good size. But stem rot destroyed Morel in the end. He gave up his nursery in despair and turned to garden design. He gave his seedlings to William Robinson and Ernest Markham before World War I. These seedlings gave a loud echo to his work for they produced varieties such as 'Abundance', 'Little Nell', 'Huldine', 'Minuet' and 'Ernest Markham', in the hands of others.

'FLORE PLENO' (syn. 'Mary Rose')

This is a plant you either love or hate. The old writers were not enthusiastic about it. The very dark colour repels some. It is a matter of the right display. Against a light background you come across an intriguing slatey cloud that compels attention. Eye-catching in the right flower arrangement.

The Warship 'Mary Rose'

This great ship was built by Henry VIII for the British fleet in about 1509 and rebuilt in 1536. Awaiting the French Fleet off Portsmouth in 1545, she capsized and sank with few survivors as soon as she opened fire. Too many men aboard had caused a tilting which let water in through the gun ports.

What is the link with *Clematis* 'Flore Pleno'? This clematis too was lost. A customer of the resourceful Barry Fretwell of Peveril Nursery, Devon, mentioned an unusual clematis growing on the wall of a friend's house. Mr Fretwell inspected it and describes the stems 'as akin to a tree trunk'. He identified it as the old 'Double Purple Virgin's Bower'. This was in 1981 and shortly, in 1982, the world saw the raising of the ship 'Mary Rose' from the waters of the Solent, UK. He linked both momentous events by suggesting the name of 'Mary Rose' for the rediscovered sixteenth century clematis.

Name Meaning double flower (syn. 'Mary Rose'). Common Names: 'Double Purple Virgin's Bower' (*Hortus Kewensis* 1789), *Clematis caerulea* 'Flore Pleno' (Gerard's *Herball* 1597). *Clematis altera* 'Flore Pleno'(Clusius).

Origin A very old viticella and introduced to England in 1569 by Mr Hugh Morgan and said to be a native of Spain and Italy (Hortus Kewensis 1789). Described by John Gerard in his *Herball* of 1597 and John Parkinson in his *Paradisi* of 1629. Also included in Philip Miller's *The Gardener's Dictionary* of 1768, *Hortus Kewensis* (Aiton) of 1789, *The Botanic Garden* (Maund) of 1825-26, and *Arboretum et Fruticetum* (Loudon) of 1838. Dr Jules le Bel (*The Garden*, 16 July 1898) said it was still in cultivation at that time in France. Listed by Whitehead in his book *Clematis* in 1968. Rediscovered by Barry Fretwell of Peveril Nursery, Devon, UK, in 1981.

Habit Deciduous. Climber. Vigorous to 3.5m (12ft). Very profuse flowerer. Hardy. Flowers mid-summer to early autumn. Any aspect.

Flower Round flower up to 6cm (2in); colour is dark blue and can appear almost black; flower is supported by 4 mid-violet (lighter at base) tepals which fall off as flower matures; rest of flower is mass of sterile purple petaloid stamens which open layer by layer and fall off as flower matures; on firm stalks.

Foliage Mid-green. Usually 5 leaflets of 3 lobes.

Special Features Good for flower arrangements.

'HENDERSONII'

This is an old and famous plant as it was a most noteworthy cross between two clematis species as far back as 1835. Not tall nor a strong climber but a wonderful clamberer over supports or shrubs. The dancing bells keep coming over a long period. Makes lovely small cut flowers. Useful container plant.

Name After the raiser.

Origin Raised by J.A. Henderson of Pineapple Nursery, Edgware Road, London, in 1835. Flowered in the garden of a Mr Chandler of Vauxhall, London, and hence also got the name of *C. chandleri*. Cross between *C. integrifolia* and *C. viticella*.

Habit Deciduous. Weak climber. Semi shrub. Vigorous. Grows to 2m (6½ft). Profusion of flowers produced continuously over a long period from mid-summer to early autumn.

Flower Bell-shaped flower; up to 4cm (1½in) long and 5cm (2in) diameter at first; opens later to flower 9cm (3½in) across; 4 tepals that recurve and twist at the tips; dark mauve colour to inside of tepals with rosy-mauve central bar; serrated edges; mauve reverse with central deep mauve bar; yellow anther with greeny-yellow filament; off-white carpels; flowers on long firm stalks. Said by W.J. Bean in his *Wall Shrubs and Hardy Climbers* (1939) to be slightly perfumed.

Foliage Pinnate with 5-7 segments.

Special Features A container plant. Useful for cutting. Compare with 'Blue Boy' (earlier) and 'Eriostemon' (Supplementary list). Darker flower than 'Blue Boy'.

George Jackman and 'Hendersonii'

When George Jackman stepped out into his father's nursery one day in 1858 at Woking, England, one of the flowers in bloom was 'Hendersonii'. His eye caught sight of two other bloomers, *C. lanuginosa*, a beautiful large immigrant from China, and *C. viticella* 'Atrorubens'. He pondered on crossing the three of them. He made two crosses, *C. lanuginosa* x *C. viticella* 'Atrorubens' and *C. lanuginosa* x 'Hendersonii'. Both crosses produced seedlings but one from the viticella cross stole the show, it was the famous *C.* 'Jackmanii'.

'HULDINE'

'Huldine' has a large following for the exceptional beauty of the flower. It is also fine for flower arrangements. An unusual attribute is that it looks lovely from behind. Flowering late it extends the period of flowering of the viticellas and has been reported in bloom as late as early winter.

Name Meaning is said to be a continental name. May be associated with 'Grace', which would certainly fit the flower. Presumably named by William Robinson in 1934, long after it was received from Morel.

Origin Came from the seedlings given to William Robinson and Ernest Markham by Francisque Morel before 1914. Introduced in 1934 by Ernest Markham.

Habit Deciduous. Climber. Vigorous. Grows to 4.5m (15ft). Profuse flowerer. Flowers late mid-summer to late autumn. Any aspect.

Flower Open, upward-looking flower; to 10cm (4in) in size; usually 6 tepals with no overlay and slightly reflexed from midway in tepal; colour of tepals white tinged violet with more violet at edges in young flowers; back has attractive rosy violet bar down centre; anthers yellow-green; filament white; prominent off-white pistil; firm long stems.

Foliage 5 leaflets. Mid-green.

Special Features Award of Merit, Royal Horticultural Society, 1934, granted to William Robinson. Excellent cut flower.

Do You Look At the Back of Your Clematis Flower?

You may well be surprised if you do. 'Huldine' is a case in point. Looking at a bud dancing in the breeze the light often catches the lovely rosy velvet bar on the back of each tepal. In a flower arrangement it matters little which way the flower points as back or front is attractive. Another viticella with a lovely back is 'Venosa Violacea'. Look at the backs of your Large-Flowered clematis too.

'JENNY CADDICK'

This is a handsome new introduction. It has a neat, clean, glowing pinky-red flower. Medium-sized flowers come in succession over a long period into mid-autumn. It has a promising future.

Name After the daughter of the introducer, Harry Caddick.

Origin Received as a seedling from a customer by Mr Harry Caddick of Caddick's Nursery, Thelwall, Warrington, Cheshire, UK and introduced in 1996.

Habit Deciduous. Climber. Vigorous. Grows to 3m (10ft). Profuse flowerer in successive bloomings. Flowers mid-summer to mid-autumn. Any aspect.

Flower Semi-nodding bell at first, it soon opens flat to make a flower of up to 8cm (3¼in); tepals 4-6 - crumpled along edge and dark glowing pinky-red in colour; lighter colour on each side of tepal centre; serrated edges; back of tepal is silvery red with a lighter central bar; anther yellow; prominent green connective; white filament; creamy prominent pistil.

Foliage 5 entire leaflets. Neat. Mid-green.

Do You Look at the Ground?

You may, of course, pick up a Roman coin, or a gold bracelet. If you look at the ground under your clematis you may strike gold too. Someone saw a seedling of 'Jenny Caddick' and the expert identified its promise. But do not be over hopeful. Probably only one in a thousand will prove a winner. Yet some lovely viticellas came to us this way: 'Betty Corning', 'Margaret Hunt', 'Prince Charles'. Every spring when I look at *C. montana* 'Freda' I applaud the initiative of Jim Fisk in spotting that it was gold.

'KERMESINA'

A very popular plant. Makes an instant appeal to some viewers. They exclaim with pleasure when they see the dark centre against the red. Very reliable grower. Small blooms produce a cloud of bloom.

Name Red colour of the flower reminded the raiser of the kermes insect (*Chermes ilicis*) from which the red dye cochineal is obtained.

Origin Raised by M. Lemoine in his nursery at Nancy, France, and introduced in 1883. One of three bred by him at that time, the others being 'Venosa Violacea' and 'Grandiflora' (see *The Garden*, February 1883, p.124). 'Kermesina' said to be a seedling from 'Venosa' (NB, not 'Venosa Violacea').

Habit Deciduous. Climber. Very vigorous. Grows to 6m (20ft). Very profuse flowerer. Flowers mid-summer to mid-autumn. Any aspect.

Flower Semi-nodding at first; opens to a flower up to 10cm (4in) across; 4-5 tepals that may twist but do not overlap; colour of tepals is a dusky crimson with a central white bar more prominent at base; back has a white green-ridged central bar; serrated edge; anther is red-brown and filament green; a prominent pistil is maroon-black; centre of plant looks dark to the viewer

Foliage 5 leaflets with 3 lobes. Small leaves. Dark green.

Special Features Compare with 'Madame Julia Correvon' that has a light centre and flowers earlier.

Confusion in the Reds

It is generally accepted that the red described above is the 'Kermesina' raised by Lemoine, but there is another not dissimilar red by the name of 'Rubra'.

Gerard talks of 'Rubra' ('Red Flowered Ladies Bower') in his *Herball* of 1597 as does John Parkinson of 'Flore Rubro' in his *Paradisi* of 1629. 'Rubra', a single red, was listed in Philip Miller's *Dictionary* of 1768 and by Weston in 1774. 'Rubra-Grandiflora' is listed by Moore and Jackman in their *Clematis* of 1877, describing it as a desirable claret-crimson flower with green stamens. *Index Londinensis* lists 'Rubra-Grandiflora' in 1930. It was also listed by Whitehead in the second edition of *Clematis* in 1968. It may still be around.

'KOSMICZESKAJA MELODIJA'

Your reaction to this flower depends on your liking for dark red flowers. This is probably the darkest in the viticella group (except for 'Black Prince' in the Supplementary List). Some are ecstatic about them. Some not. It is good to find a Russian clematis being accepted worldwide and more will follow.

Name Means – 'Cosmic Melody' and celebrates Russian first entry into space.

Origin Raised by A.N. Volosenko-Valensis and M.A. Beskaravainaja at the State Nikita Botanical Gardens at Yalta, Crimea, in 1965. It came from a cross between 'Gipsy Queen' and 'Jackmanii Alba'.

Habit Deciduous. Climber. Very vigorous. Grows to 3.5m (12ft). Profuse flowering. Flowers early summer to early autumn. Any aspect.

Flower Open flower up to 9cm (3½in); 4-6 tepals, gappy, no overlap; colour of tepals is deep red mauve; back has light violet colour with violet bar at centre; anther purple fading to brown; white filament; off-white prominent pistil.

Foliage 5 leaflets. Pinnate.

Why Not Start at Seventy

For a very long time hybridising had been going on in the old USSR. One centre was Leningrad which has a fine botanic garden. *C. maximowicziana* (now called *C. terniflora*) was named after one of its director plant hunters. The main centre, perhaps because of its climate, was at Yalta, in the Crimea. Here distinguished hybridists were A.N. Volosenko-Valensis and M.A. Beskaravainaja. They bred 'Kosmiczeskaja Melodija'. M. Orlov was active in Kiev in the Ukraine,

The most unusual hybridising was going on in Moscow. Here at the age of 70 Mrs Sharonova, an amateur, started her hybridising. She continued until her death in 1987 at the age of 102! She was renowned for the brilliant colouring of her Large Flowered clematis; these are beginning to filter round the world.

'LITTLE NELL'

This is a classic viticella – vigorous, reliable, and prolific. Covered with thousands of flowers of the most delicate beauty that you can imagine. Study the bloom carefully. Is it not a thing of great subdued beauty? Will grow on a north aspect if need be. Cut for an exquisite little bouquet.

Name Named after Ernest Markham's wife, Nell.

Origin One of the seedlings raised by Morel about 1900 and given by him to William Robinson and Ernest Markham at Gravetye Manor, Sussex, UK before 1914. In turn given by Ernest Markham to Jackman of Woking who introduced it about 1939.

Habit Deciduous. Climber. Very vigorous. Grows to 6m (20ft). Very profuse flowerer. Flowers from early summer to early autumn. Any aspect.

Flower Semi-nodding at first it soon opens flat; makes a flower up to 7cm (2½in) across; 4-6 tepals that may recurve and twist at tips; the central area of tepals are white and the edges pinky-violet; central area of back of tepal is white and is greener near base with violet edges; anther is dark green and filament is light green; prominent pistil is off-white; flowers on long stalks.

Foliage Usually 5 leaflets of 3 lobes.

The Predominantly White Viticellas

'Predominantly' is important as white in viticellas often proves to be a white tinged with violet. Violet is really the basic colour of clematis for it is never far away in varying degrees. 'Huldine' is the queen of the whites for its size, strong stems and being eye-catching back and front. For drama of course there is 'Alba-Luxurians'; ask your friends to view it in the garden, or have a bloom on your dinner table. Have they ever seen a flower like that? If your friends admire quiet beauty then 'Little Nell' is for them. 'Minuet' and 'Tango' are 'pretty' by any standards. For fascination there is white and purple 'Venosa Violacea'. Every bloom is different, each has a face, and each face seems to want to talk to you (page 66).

'MADAME JULIA CORREVON'

This is an ever-popular viticella. Its appeal is the glowing red colour, its interestingly twisted tepals and light centre. Very reliable. Excellent patio plant, especially in the ground. Prune after first flowering and it will produce a second crop of flowers into the autumn.

Name Named by Morel, the raiser, after a member of the Correvon family of nurserymen.

Origin Bred by Francisque Morel of Lyon-Vaise, France, by crossing a viticella with his new clematis 'Ville de Lyon' which he introduced in 1899. Introduced in 1900 and reported in *Revue Horticole* of that year.

Habit Deciduous. Climber. Very vigorous. Climbs to 3.5m (12ft). Profuse flowerer. Flowers early summer to early autumn. Any aspect.

Flower Makes open flower up to 13cm (5in); 4-6 tepals that do not overlap but may recurve and twist at tip; gappy flower; tepals are rosy red, lighter at base; serrated edges; back of tepals a light red especially at centre; anthers greeny-yellow; filaments white, prominent; pistil off-white, prominent; strong stems.

Foliage Usually 5 leaflets of 3 lobes.

Special Features Can be used in containers and for cutting. Award of Garden Merit, Royal Horticultural Society.

The Choice of Red Clematis

Spoilt for choice you might say. For early flowering, and pruning for a second crop, try 'Madame Julia Correvon' and strong growing 'Södertälje'. For late flowering and extending the season of flowering try 'Royal Velours' and 'Ville de Lyon'. The brightest red and the largest bloom comes with 'Ville de Lyon'. The lightest reds are 'Abundance', 'Madame Julia Correvon' and 'Jenny Caddick'. 'Kermesina' looks dark for its dark centre but the tepals are bright. Mid-red is 'Södertälje'. The dark reds are 'Royal Velours' and 'Kosmiczeskaja Melodija'. Which is the most attractive? I would not dare to say (see page 71).

'MARGARET HUNT'

A fine viticella for its beautiful pink flowers of unusual, attractive shade of pink, which is difficult to describe. Flowers keep coming over a long period. This is a plant to brighten up a dark corner or dark shrubs.

Name After the raiser.

Origin A seedling in the garden of Mrs Margaret Hunt of Norwich, Norfolk, UK and which grew to a large plant. It was seen by Jim Fisk of Fisk's Clematis Nursery, Westleton, Suffolk, UK who introduced it in 1969.

Habit Deciduous. Climber. Vigorous. Grows to 3.5m (12ft). Any aspect. Flowers early summer to early autumn.

Flower Open flower up to 12cm (4in); 4-6 tepals with no overlap; tepals are rosy-pink fading to light pink with slightly deeper colour at centre; back of tepals pale pink with deeper pink at centre and around edge; anthers brown; filaments greeny-white; pistil off-white, prominent; firm stalk.

Foliage 5 leaflets - entire. Light green.

Special Features Compare with 'Margot Koster' which is a deeper colour (page 72). A container plant. Suitable for cutting.

The Great Introducer

'Margaret Hunt' was introduced by Jim Fisk, one of many clematis introduced by him. Jim, though also a hybridist, has a remarkable eye for a good plant. He sought out distinctive plants from England, Poland, Japan, the American continent, New Zealand – the world. He was the first Englishman to start a nursery growing clematis alone. Way back – he is an octogenarian – he was first acquainted with clematis through his aunt's 'Jackmanii'. Then he became a propagator. After World War II he became the village postman while his clematis nursery grew. His innovative work brought clematis back to cultivation. His clematis appeared in his books and remarkable displays at the Chelsea Shows in London.

'MARGOT KOSTER'

This plant scores with its continuous flowering over a long period. Flowers into mid-autumn. Colour is a most appealing pink. Suitable for a container. Grow against dark foliage and backgrounds. Stunning against the almost black-leaved version of the smoke tree (*Cotinus*).

Name After member of family of the raiser.

Origin Raised at the Koster Nursery, Boskoop, Holland, and introduced in 1911.

Habit Deciduous. Climber. Vigorous. Grows to 3m (10ft). Profuse flowerer. Flowers continuously from early summer to mid-autumn. Any aspect.

Flower Open flower up to 12cm (4in); 4-6 tepals that do not overlap; tepals may twist or recurve at tip or edges; bright pink colour; serrated edges; back of tepals are paler pink; anthers yellow; filament white; pistil off-white.

Foliage 5 leaflets - entire. Large.

Special Features Compare with another pink, 'Margaret Hunt' that is paler (page 72). Suitable for container.

The Trials of the Hybridiser

Most of our viticellas are the result of very hard work over a long period of time by dedicated hybridisers. The greater the discovery the greater the reaction of critics. It happens in all fields. At first there is a denial of the discovery. That was Alphonse Lavallée's reaction to George Jackman's 'Jackmanii'. Jackman had never hybridised it and instead had imported *Clematis hakonensis* from Japan! It was soon proved that Jackman had not known *Clematis hakonensis*. It was also refuted because in France, at Metz, Simon Louis, soon after Jackman, had made a very similar cross (*C. lanuginosa* x a different viticella) and produced a plant akin to Jackman's, *C.* 'Splendida'. Next reaction is to say 'if it's true then let's take it over'. A neighbouring nurseryman to Jackman announced that he was producing large quantities of Large Flowered clematis. When challenged he said he had so many because he sowed seeds in the autumn and in the spring they came up in quantity. That was his undoing. By then it was known that the seeds of Large Flowered clematis take two years or more to germinate. Investigation showed he had worked with Jackman on his seedlings and had thought it profitable to leave taking seedlings with him!

'MINUET'

A very pretty flower which never fails to attract and bring light and colour into the garden. Brilliant over dark shrubs and trees. Lovely dancing in a wind, hence perhaps, its name. Very reliable - a classic viticella.

Name No certainty why Markham chose this name. We can conjecture he was impressed by the pretty spectacle of its dance in a breeze.

Origin Bred by Francisque Morel of Lyon-Vaise, France, about 1900 and one of the seedlings given to William Robinson and Ernest Markham at Gravetye Manor, Sussex, UK. Named by Ernest Markham and introduced by Jackman's of Woking after 1930.

Habit Deciduous. Climber. Very vigorous. Grows up to 3m (10ft). Profuse flowerer. Any aspect.

Flower May be a semi-nodding bell at first but soon makes an open rather square flower up to 8cm (3¼in); 4 tepals with small overlap at base and some twisting and recurving of the tips and edges; centre of tepal is white with mauvy-red veins while the edges have a band of mauvy-red; wavy edges; back of tepal is pale mauvy-red, with central ridges; anther mauve, fading to brown; filament green; pistil dark mauve and prominent feature of the flower; long thin stalks.

Foliage 5-7 leaflets ovate, entire. Mid-green.

Special Features Award of Garden Merit, Royal Horticultural Society. Compare with 'Tango' and 'Foxtrot', all with musical associations (Chapter Four, Supplementary List of Viticellas).

'Minuet and Tango'

These musical cousins are very similar despite one being bred by Morel about 1900 and the other very recently by Barry Fretwell. Nonetheless you will want to grow both as there are differences, the chief being in the colour round the edge of the flowers: mauve-red in 'Minuet' and cherry-red in 'Tango'. There may also be a greater area of colour in 'Tango' despite being a slightly smaller flower. The tepals may be more likely to twist and recurve in 'Minuet'. The pistil is darker in 'Minuet' (page 70).

'MRS T. LUNDELL'

This is an exciting newcomer. Most blooms of clematis get duller with time but this one gets more colourful. Blooms also twist and curve most attractively. The ruffled surface adds to the attraction. May have the loveliest colouring in the group. Fine for cutting.

Name After wife of distinguished Swedish hybridist.

Origin Raised by Tage Lundell. Named after his death when introduced in 1985 by Krister Cedergren of Helsingborg, Sweden.

Habit Deciduous. Climber. Vigorous. Grows to 4.5m (12ft). Profuse flowerer over long period from early summer to early autumn.

Flower Semi-nodding bell at first; it opens to a cross-shaped flower up to 12.5cm (4½in); 4 tepals that curve, recurve and twist most attractively; colour of inside of tepal is mauve with rosy-mauve central bar of deeper colour at the tip and white at base; back of tepal is mauve with central dark mauve bar that fades with time. Ruffled surface; anther light yellow; filament green; pistil greeny-white, prominent; on long stalks.

Foliage 3-5 leaflets, solitary or lobed. Mid-green.

Special Features Compare with 'Abundance'. Has same ruffled surface but much more colour and tepals twist and curve. Suitable for cutting.

A Sad Tale

'Mrs T. Lundell' was named after the wife of Mr Tage Lundell. Tage Lundell, with Magnus Johnson and Jan Lindmark, was one of the three distinguished hybridists of Sweden. He was a customs officer by profession at Helsingborg and thus an amateur. At least three of his Large Flowered clematis are widely grown: 'Corona' (1955), 'Dawn' (1960) and 'Serenata' (1960). Then stem rot struck; it may have arrived on an imported plant. Tage Lundell gave up growing clematis. Stem rot vanquished the great Morel also. Tage Lundell died in 1985.

'PAGODA'

The lovely hanging bells of this plant together with its continuous flowering make it a most desirable plant. Non-stop flowering throughout its season. Looks well on a support that allows it to hang down to the ground or clambering over low shrubs. Useful container plant.

Name Suggested by shape of flower.

Origin Raised by John Treasure, of Treasures of Tenbury, at Tenbury Wells, Worcestershire, UK, and introduced in 1980. Cross of *C. viticella* x *C. viticella* 'Etoile Rose'.

Habit Deciduous. Climber. Vigorous. Grows to 2m (8ft). Profuse flowerer. Flowers continuously from mid-summer to early autumn. Any aspect.

Flower Nodding bell-shaped flower up to 12cm (4½in); 4 tepals that flare and may twist at tips and showing mottling; inside of tepal is reddish-purple colour which is stronger in outer two-thirds and white at base; on outer side strong purple bar down centre of tepal and pale pink margins; anther yellow-green; filament green; pistil green, prominent; bracts below flower.

Foliage 7 leaflets of 3 lobes.

Special Features Raiser claimed it for Texensis group but nodding nature of flowers, the foliage, and ancestry make it clearly a viticella. Useful for containers.

Burford House Gardens

John Treasure bred 'Pagoda' with many other clematis and displayed them in this beautiful garden on a river bank in the west of England. A fine garden for seeing clematis well displayed. John Treasure, an architect, turned to gardening at the age of fifty-two and thereafter devoted himself to the garden, his nursery, and hybridising. He bred *C.* 'Fireworks', *C. tangutica* 'Burford Variety', and *C.* 'Royalty'. 'Pagoda' may well prove to be his finest introduction. He died in 1993 at the age of eighty-two.

'POLISH SPIRIT'

A very vigorous late-flowering viticella with a lovely velvety flower. Dark colouring is relieved by rosy bar. Flowers into the autumn and extends the flowering period of the viticellas. Too strong for a container but wonderful over light-leaved or light-flowered plants and shrubs. Glorious in the willow-leafed pear (*Pyrus salicifolia* 'Pendula').

Name Reminder of its Polish origin.

Origin Hybridised by Brother Stefan Franczak, of Warsaw, Poland, and introduced in 1990 by Raymond Evison of the Guernsey Clematis Nursery Ltd.

Habit Deciduous. Climber. Very vigorous. Height to 4.5m (15ft). Flowers mid-summer to mid-autumn. Any aspect.

Flower Horizontal open flower up to 9cm (3½in); 4 or 5 tepals with no overlap; rich purple colour to tepals with rosy-purple central bar; velvety texture; serrated edges; outside of tepal is lighter purple with central white-purple bar; anthers rosy-purple; filament greeny-white; pistil off-white, prominent; on long stalks.

Foliage 5 leaflets, small, entire.

Special Features Award of Garden Merit, Royal Horticultural Society. Compare with 'Etoile Violette' and 'Blue Belle'.

Three Dark Blue Viticellas

In the viticella group we have three outstanding dark purple clematis, the English 'Blue Belle', the French 'Etoile Violette', and the Polish 'Polish Spirit'. 'Etoile Violette' flowers early unlike the other two which flower late. 'Blue Belle' has the darkest colouring but this is relieved by a light centre. There is a light centre also to 'Etoile Violette'. Though 'Polish Spirit' has a dark centre the dark purple colouring is relieved by a rosy bar. 'Etoile Violette' is vigorous but the other two are outstandingly vigorous (page 73).

'PRINCE CHARLES'

Becoming a very popular plant since it joined 'Perle d'Azur' in the uncommon light blue category. Produces a mass of bloom. More compact than 'Perle d'Azur' and so can be used in a smaller garden. Lovely against dark backgrounds and with flowering yellow and pink roses. Try it with rose 'Summer Wine' for a lesson in elegant delicate beauty

Name After His Royal Highness Prince Charles of the British and Commonwealth Royal Family.

Origin Seedling given to Alister Keay, St Martin's, Christchurch, New Zealand in the 1950s. Introduced to Europe by Jim Fisk in 1986 who also obtained permission to use the name.

Habit Deciduous. Climber. Vigorous. Grows to 3.5m (12ft). Profuse continuous flowerer. Flowers from early summer to early autumn. Any aspect.

Flower May be semi-nodding at first but soon presents an open flower up to 10cm (4in) across; no overlap of 4-6 tepals but they may twist; tepals are coloured violet with slight central deeper colour and tinged with red towards tip; ruffled surface; at back of tepal marked ridged white bar; anther yellow; filament green; pistil off-white, prominent.

Foliage 3-7 leaflets; 1 or 3 lobes.

Special Features Suitable for container and cutting. Compare with 'Perle d'Azur', 'Blekitny Aniol' and 'Emilia Plater'.

Naming a Viticella

It is not as easy as it seems. To start with you must avoid using a name already in vogue. Avoid a name used in the past; an old plant may return to haunt you. One can start with oneself – Margaret Hunt is a case in point. A member of the family can be remembered; the wife of Ernest Markham inspired the affectionate 'Little Nell' and a daughter inspired 'Jenny Caddick'. It can compliment a friend or the wife of a friend, 'Mrs T. Lundell'. It can note a client, 'Betty Corning', or a royal personage, 'Prince Charles'. An attempt can be made to describe a feature of the plant, 'Abundance', 'Etoile Violette' (violet star), 'Pagoda' (from its shape), 'Royal Velours' (from its texture) or even a detailed description, 'Triternata' (thrice ternate), 'Rubromarginata' (red margined). It can commemorate a town, 'Ville de Lyon', or an event, 'Kosmiczeskaja Melodija' (launch of the first Russian cosmonaut).

'PURPUREA PLENA ELEGANS'

This is a popular curiosity for its multi-tepaled structure. It is vigorous and eye-catching. Grow climbing into light shrubs and trees. Good for cutting.

Name An elegant double purple.

Origin Raised by Francisque Morel of Lyon-Vaise, France. Introduced by him in 1899. Not introduced by Edouard André as sometimes claimed. André described it in *Revue Horticole* of 1899 and gave Morel as the raiser.

Habit Deciduous. Climber. Vigorous. Grows to 3.5m (12ft). Flowers mid-summer to mid-autumn. Any aspect.

Flower Rosette-shaped up to 7cm (2½in); flower supported by 4-6 large outer tepals which drop off as flower opens leaving sterile petaloid stamens - these open row by row and may recurve; colour of flower is mauvy-red, almost maroon; tips of outer tepals may be green and there may be white at base.

Foliage 5 leaflets of 3 lobes. Light green.

Special Features Award of Garden Merit, Royal Horticultural Society. Not to be confused with 'Purpurea Plena' also raised by Morel and described in *Revue Horticole* of 1899, nor with 'Flore Pleno', described earlier (page 46). The latter is the old European double described in the early herbals. Not to be confused also with 'Purpurea Elegans' bred by Cripps in England in 1874.

A Husband and Wife Team

There must be several partnerships at work. Sylvia and Vince Denny did not raise the double clematis mentioned above, but they were responsible for a superb very popular double clematis, *C. montana* 'Broughton Star'. Amongst many Large Flowered clematis raised by them is the lovely double white 'Sylvia Denny'. Vince, a retired station master, is amateur and professional in one. The Dennys are now turning their attention to viticellas. 'Shauford', 'Sturminster' and 'Vanessa' are on our Supplementary List and will soon be generally available.

'ROYAL VELOURS'

This is a clematis for those who love deep red, almost black, colouring. A velvety sheen adds to its attraction. Needs light background and light and silvery foliage to be seen at its best.

Name Describes the velvety nature of the flower surface.

Origin Raised by Francisque Morel about 1900 and one of the seedlings given by Morel to William Robinson and Ernest Markham before 1914. Named and shown to Royal Horticultural Society by William Robinson in 1934. Shown again to RHS in 1948 and given Award of Merit by unanimous vote.

Habit Deciduous. Climber. Vigorous. Grows to 3.5m (12ft). Profuse flowerer. Any aspect. Flowers mid-summer to mid-autumn.

Flower Semi-nodding open flower up to 9cm (3½in); 4-6 tepals that slightly overlap at base; rich dark red sheen to tepals; almost black at first opening. Serrated edges back of tepals are lighter colour with central darker bar; anthers dark purple; filament green; pistil dark mauvy-red; firm stems.

Foliage 3-5 leaflets of 3 lobes.

Special Features Award of Garden Merit, Royal Horticultural Society. Compare with another dark red, 'Kosmiczeskaja Melodija'. Suitable for cutting.

The House of Jackman

As we ponder on the work that makes these beautiful clematis we come continually across the name of Jackman. The Jackman Nursery was started at Woking, Surrey, UK by William Jackman (1763-1840). When 'Jackmanii' was hybridised in 1858 there were two George Jackmans at the nursery, George senior (1801-1869) and George junior (1837-1887). It was George junior, aged twenty-one, who made the famous cross. After 'Jackmanii' came on the scene fame was assured. The Jackman displays of clematis at shows were greeted with great enthusiasm. Once stem rot struck after 1880 production was scaled down although they still produced the famous Wokingensis Texensis Group. They did not go into viticellas like Morel. Arthur Jackman (1866-1926) followed George. He was followed by Percy Jackman (1873-1934) and George Rowland Jackman (1902-1976). Plants other than clematis were always sold by the nursery. Rowland Jackman sold the business on his retirement and it became, and still is, a garden centre. (See Gauntlett, Pamela. (1995) *Jackmans of Woking*. Y Lolfa Cyf, Talybont, Wales – a book by Pamela, Rowland Jackman's daughter.)

'SÖDERTÄLJE'

This is one of the giants of the viticella world, being a very vigorous grower to 5m (16ft). Competes with 'Polish Spirit' and 'Blue Belle'. Unlike those two blue viticellas this one is red. Corrugated surface is reminiscent of 'Abundance' but it is a deeper red. Grow against light foliage and objects.

Name After the town where the raiser, Magnus Johnson, has his nursery.

Origin Introduced by Magnus Johnson at Södertälje, Sweden, in 1952 from seeds of *C. viticella* 'Grandiflora Sanguinea'. A 100 year old plant is in the Botanic Garden, Stockholm.

Habit Deciduous. Climber. Very vigorous. Grows to 5m (16ft). Flowers early summer to early autumn. Any aspect.

Flower Semi-nodding flower to 10cm (4in); 4-6 tepals that do not overlap, making gappy flower; tepals are dark purple-red; corrugated surface; serrated edges; back of tepals lighter red; anther yellow-green; filament green; pistil greeny-white, and very prominent.

Foliage 7 leaflets of 3 lobes.

Champion of the North

Magnus Johnson is an inspiration to every clematarian, world-wide. Vastly experienced, scholarly, erudite and with a background in horticulture and taxonomy, he began his interest in clematis in 1947 by building up a collection of clematis from cuttings. Many of his Large Flowered clematis from seedlings, rather than planned crossings, are well known: 'Anna', 'Cassiopeia', 'Moonlight', 'Titania', etc. 'Neodynamia' came from a planned crossing. His interest soon turned to the Small Flowered clematis, especially the alpinas where he made his major hybridising contribution. He has also taken an interest in the viticellas. In addition to his 'Södertälje' on our Supplementary List (Chapter 4) there is 'Carmencita', 'Doggy', and 'Nana'. In time for his 90th birthday he produced a massive reference work *Slaktet Klematis* (The Genus Clematis) describing all known clematis.

'TANGO'

Will inevitably be compared to 'Minuet'. 'Tango' is a slightly more colourful dancer, but 'Minuet' twists beautifully. Both are lovely, desirable, plants and a tribute to two great hybridists, Morel and Fretwell. You will end up growing both!

Name Presumably musical theme to partner 'Minuet'.

Origin Hybridised by Barry Fretwell at Peveril Nursery, Devon, UK and introduced in 1986.

Habit Deciduous. Climber. Vigorous. Grows to 3m (10ft). Profuse flowerer. Flowers mid-summer to early autumn. Any aspect.

Flower Open slightly rounded flower to 5cm (2in); 4-5 tepals; cherry-red colour takes up most of tepal with cherry-red veins on the rest; back of tepal is pale cherry-red with paler bar down centre; anther mauvy-red fading to brown; filament mid-green; pistil dark purple, prominent; long thin stalks.

Foliage 5-7 leaflets with 3 lobes. Mid-green.

Special Features Fine foliage. Compare with 'Minuet' (page 70).

An Artist at Work

In what I imagine is a leafy dell in Devon, England, one of the most successful hybridists today is at work. This is Barry Fretwell. *C. viticella* 'Tango' was one of his creations. 'Brocade' is on the Supplementary list and will soon be generally available. Fascinating *C. viticella* 'Elvan' is another. Barry Fretwell has the attractive trait of underestimating his own creations in his writings. Many of today's new Large Flowered hybrids are his; 'Peveril Pearl', for instance, is a beauty. Daringly he worked on the texensis group and gave us 'Princess Diana' and 'Ladybird Johnson'. Is vibrant, glowing, luminous 'Princess Diana' his greatest creation? He disagrees and has named his finest hybrid after his wife 'Patricia Ann Fretwell' – a lovely tribute to the other member of the team.

'TRITERNATA RUBROMARGINATA'

This is a plant for every garden. Makes a small cloud of colour in a bed. It is wonderful climbing over dark foliage. Plant near a path or gate to savour its overwhelming scent. You do not have to look for this plant; it finds you with its scent.

Name Thrice ternate leaves and red margined flower.

Origin *C. flammula* x *C. viticella* 'Rubra' the cross made in 1862 by Cripps & Son of Tunbridge Wells, Kent, England.

Habit Deciduous. Climber. Very vigorous. Height to 5m (16ft). Very profuse flowerer. Flowers early summer to early autumn. Any aspect. Hardier than the parent *C. flammula*.

Flower Star-like bloom up to 5cm (2in); 4 tepals that curl and twist especially in tip area; tepal is bright mauve-red for two-thirds of its length; rest white; back of tepal is mauve with white central area, especially towards base; anther pale yellow; filament green; pistil cream; produced along stalk in pairs or cymes; strong almond fragrance.

Foliage 5-7 leaflets which are either lobed or cleft. Small. Mid-green.

Colour and Scent

How difficult these are to describe. The colour changes can depend on climate. In general the more sun the stronger the colour initially. With time the sun fades the flower and colour can change dramatically. The maturity of a flower is another factor: usually the younger the flower the stronger the colour. Time of the year influences matters too. Both in spring and autumn less light can bring a green tinge to a flower; 'Alba Luxurians' is a dramatic example of this. To describe a colour also has its problems. There are a few colour charts; each number on the cards has a meaning for the designer of the cards but not to anyone else. Biggest problems are the deep blues so common to clematis. Experts even have different ideas of mauve, purple, violet, lavender, indigo, etc.

As for scent there appears to be no agreed way of defining fragrance. To say 'pleasant' tells you nothing. So scents are compared to another flower such as lavender, or a plant like mint, a tree like hawthorn, to a fruit like lemon, to an animal scent like musk, or seeds such as ginger, or to a familiar synthetic product like chocolate. Sometimes the best we can do is to indicate strength such as weak, strong, very strong or even overwhelming, like 'Triternata Rubromarginata'.

'VENOSA VIOLACEA'

An exceptional plant with colouring that is rather different from the rest of viticellas. Flowers are deeply veined, as the name suggests. Most intriguing is that the colourings of the blooms vary from one to another. Thus the plant has flowers with different faces that appear to want to talk to you. They flower early and if pruned after flowering a second crop is possible. Has an attractive back to the flower. Excellent for cutting and for a container.

His Nickname was 'Clematis'

For tracing the ancestry of plants, as you can see here, you need records. A great recorder was the American Joel Elias Spingarn. He came to England in 1927, caught the clematis fever and his enthusiasm was so great that he was nicknamed 'Clematis'. He was also known as 'Mr Clematis, America' and 'The Clematis King'. He admitted to being 'a maniac about clematis'. He founded a large collection in his home 'Troutbeck', Dutchess County, NY. He documented the history of the American clematis and contributed to books by Ernest Markham and Stanley Whitehead.

That was not all. He was President of the National Association for the Advancement of Coloured People, a poet, literary critic, author of a number of books and a candidate for Congress. Like 'Venosa Violacea' he had a number of faces!

Name Full of veins which are 'violet'.

Origin One of three clematis of the viticella group raised by M. Lemoine of Nancy, France, and introduced in 1883. The other two were 'Kermesina' and 'Grandiflora'.

Habit Deciduous. Climber. Vigorous. Grows up to 3m (10ft). Profusion of flowers. Flowers from early summer to early autumn. Any aspect.

Flower Upright open flower of 4-6 tepals, usually 6 up to 12cm (4½in) across; tepals may be slightly recurved along length and slightly overlapping; depth of colour and amount of white may vary from flower to flower; white-veined bar at centre of tepal which is whiter near base and more reddy-mauve near tip; from bar mauve veins radiate towards edge and become blocks of mauve near edges; back of tepal is pale mauve with a distinct, reddy-mauve, ridged bar down the middle; bract half way down stalk; anther dark mauve; filament greeny-white; stigma dark mauve.

Foliage 5 leaflets, single, almost lobed. Light green.

Special Features Award of Garden Merit, Royal Horticultural Society. Suitable for cutting and for a container. Not to be confused with C. 'Venosa' which was raised by M. Krampen, of Rosskothen, near Essen, Germany in 1857. It was known as the 'Blue Veined' clematis. It was said to be a cross of an atragene *C. alpina* and *C. patens*. When reported in *Revue Horticole* of 1860 (p.184) objection, 'Graves Objections', was made to the probable parentage. *C. sieboldii* and *C. florida* were offered as alternatives. (The latter was suggested by Barry Fretwell recently for 'Venosa Violacea'.) Its ancestry produced comment in *Revue Horticole* in 1873 p.462, 1874 p.84, and in 1874 p.425.

'VILLE DE LYON'

A popular plant for its bright carmine flowers. Comparatively large for a viticella. It brings this colour into the autumn with its late flowering. An attractive container plant and for cutting. In common with some other red clematis, it tends to have brown dying leaves on the lower few feet. Hide lower part of stems with a shrub, or plant a low-growing clematis with it, or bring down a high stem to hide the lower stems.

Name Named after his home city by the hybridist.

Origin A hybrid by Francisque Morel of 33 Rue du Souvenir, Lyon-Vaise, France. A cross with the pollen of *C. coccinea* (now *C. texensis*) on a Large Flowered clematis 'Viviand Morel' (*C. viticella* 'Rosea' x *C. viticella* 'Kermesina'). Introduced in 1899. Morel put immunity to wilt down to the parent *C. coccinea*; probably correct but the viticella parentage would also contribute.

Habit Deciduous. Climber. Vigorous. Grows to 3m (10ft). Moderate profusion of flowers. Flowers continuously mid-summer to mid-autumn. Any aspect.

Flower Upright open flower to 10cm (4in); 6 tepals that overlap at base and may recurve at edges; when first open flower has even colouring; as flower matures central part becomes paler (Plate 24); tepals are carmine red; back of tepals ridged and duller red; prominent stamens; anthers yellow; filament white; pistil off-white; long stalk.

Foliage 3-5 leaflets. Lower leaflets for first 1m (3ft) may turn brown and die.

Special Features Good for a container and cutting.

Estonian Giants

Breaking new ground in Estonia is a husband and wife team, Uno and Aini Kivistik. They began to work with clematis in 1974 and to hybridise from 1979. In Estonia, in addition to their own plants, they had the clematis introduced from Yalta, Kiev, Moscow, and Leningrad. By crossing the best hybrids the Kivistiks had 4000 seeds. From these they produced many hybrid plants and from those 200 were selected for further trials. The Jackmanii Group is very important in northern countries because stems may not survive the winter; but with this group new growth is made from the ground each year. After a while the Kivistiks turned their attention to the viticellas, for the same reason. In our Supplementary list you can see how successful they have been. As the enthusiastic Latvian grower, Alvars Irbe, put it 'the Kivistiks have opened a new page in the history of world clematis breeding'.

(Sadly, Uno Kivistik died during the preparation of this book and is buried in a forest glade near his home.)

PLATE 17. Compare the three mixed white and purple bells of 'Pagan', 'Elvan' and 'Betty Corning'.

COMPARING VITICELLAS

Bell-shaped viticellas (See page 42 'Elvan')
The very small white *C. campaniflora* is a very large plant and is easy to recognise as is the large trumpet shape of 'Etoile Rose'; neither of these are represented in this photograph.

   This leaves us with the three mixed white and purple bells of, left to right in Plate 17 (above), 'Pagoda', 'Elvan' and 'Betty Corning'.

   There are two medium height viticellas with bells and on the left is the deep blue. 'Hendersonii' and on the right the lighter blue of 'Blue Boy' in Plate 18 (below).

PLATE 18. The deep blue of 'Hendersonii' (left) contrasts with the lighter blue of 'Blue Boy'.

PLATE 19. From left to right, 'Blekitny Aniol', 'Kasmu', 'Emilia Plater' and 'Prince Charles'.

Flowers with a ruffled surface (See page 43 'Emilia Plater')
From left to right in Plate 19 (above) we have 'Blekitny Aniol', 'Kasmu', 'Emilia Plater' and 'Prince Charles'.

Of the two Polish ruffled viticellas in Plate 20 (below), 'Blekitny Aniol' is a light violet and 'Emilia Plater', of a darker violet.

The predominantly white viticellas (See page 52 'Little Nell')
Each has an attractive face. In the back row of Plate 21 (page 70) is 'Little Nell', white tinged with violet at the margin, and 'Minuet', white tinged with pink. At the left of the front row is 'Alba Luxurians' with its easily recognisable green tinge. In the

PLATE 20. Compare the lighter violet colour of 'Blekitny Aniol' (left) with the darker 'Emilia Plater'.

PLATE 21. Left to right, back row, 'Little Nell' and 'Minuet'. Front row, 'Alba Luxurians', 'Huldine' and 'Venosa Violacea'.

middle of the front row is 'Huldine' with a pure white flower slightly tinged with violet. The fascinating 'Venosa Violacae', the deep purple on white, is on the right.

'Tango' and 'Minuet' are dancers but in slightly different dresses. 'Tango' on the left in Plate 22 is a brighter cherry pink and has a larger area of colour than 'Minuet' on right. (See page 56, 'Minuet').

PLATE 22. 'Tango' (left) and 'Minuet' dance together.

PLATE 23. Back row, (left to right) 'Kosmiczeskaja Melodija', 'Kermesina' and 'Royal Velours'. Front row, 'Abundance', 'Madame Julia Correvon', 'Ville de Lyon' and 'Södertälje'.

The predominantly red viticellas (See also page 53)
In the back row of Plate 23 (above) are the three deep red viticellas: 'Kosmiczeskaja Melodija' on left, 'Kermesina' in the middle and 'Royal Velours' on right. 'Kermesina' has a dark centre but the tepals are not over-dark. The front row are a light red with white centre. On the left is 'Abundance', next comes 'Madame Julia Correvon', then the medium sized flower of 'Ville de Lyon' with the very vigorous early flowering 'Södertälje' on the right.

PLATE 24. 'Ville de Lyon' shows the influence of sun and time with the lighter red of the central area of the tepal in the flower on the right.

The plate of 'Ville de Lyon', Plate 24 (page 71), shows the influence of time. An early bloom has red colouring throughout the tepal. With sun and time the more central area of the tepal becomes a lighter red (page 67, 'Ville de Lyon'). This phenomenon is seen in other clematis; it is very marked in *C. montana* 'Freda'.

Predominantly pink viticellas
The lighter pink of 'Margaret Hunt' can easily be distinguished in Plate 25 from the deeper pink of 'Margot Koster' on the right (pages 54 and 55).

The dark blue viticellas
French, early flowering, 'Etoile Violette', on the left in Plate 26 (top) has a white centre as has the English late flowering vigorous 'Blue Belle' on right. The Polish, late flowering, very vigorous 'Polish Spirit' at centre has a dark centre, but the tepals are relieved with a rosy stripe (page 59).

Double viticellas
These are easily distinguishable. 'Flore Pleno' (Syn: 'Mary Rose'), left in Plate 27 is small and grey-black. 'Purpurea Plena Elegans'(right) is larger and is lighter purple.

PLATE 25. Lighter pink ' Margaret Hunt' contrasts with darker 'Margot Koster'.

PLATE 26. Early flowering 'Etoile Violette' (left), late flowering 'Blue Belle' (right) and vigorous 'Polish Spirit' (centre).

PLATE 27. Double viticellas 'Purpurea Plena Elegans' (right) and 'Flore Pleno' (Syn. 'Mary Rose') are easily distinguishable.

PLATE 28. Rose 'Iceberg' and viticella 'Margot Koster' produce a pleasing colour combination.

PLATE 29. The world's most popular clematis, 'Perle d'Azur'.

CHAPTER THREE
Large Flowered Viticellas

The clematis in this group have blooms comparable in size to the Large Flowered Clematis. At some point an expert, or two, has put up a case for inclusion of each one in the Viticella Group. Hence their placement here.

With one noteworthy exception, 'Perle d'Azur', the varieties in this group do not produce the continuous profusion of flowers that we have seen in the small and medium flowered groups. 'Perle d'Azur' is an exceptional clematis that makes as large a display as a small montana clematis. Gardeners should include it in any collection of viticellas.

This group of large viticellas has one handicap. Not as vulnerable to stem rot (wilt) as the Early Large Flowered Group of clematis, they will still occasionally succumb. Probably not so vulnerable as to need preventative fungicides but they may need special management. Hence the inclusion of a special section for them under Cultivation later.

PLATE 30. 'Ascotiensis'.

'ASCOTIENSIS'

This plant scores for the lovely clear colour of its bloom, which does not fade. Flower colour is more vivid for its light centre. It flowers in the late autumn and is valuable for this reason. It is also excellent for cutting. The plant is good for a container.

Name After the place, Ascot, Berkshire, UK, where the plant was raised.

Origin Raised by John Standish (1814-1875) and introduced in 1871. John Standish at one time partnered another clematis raiser, Charles Noble of Bagshot. Some of Robert Fortune's plants from China were sent to Standish.

Habit Deciduous. Climbing. Fairly vigorous. Grows to 3.6m (12ft). Flowers mid-summer to early autumn. Any aspect.

Flower Upright open flower up to 15cm (6in); 4-6 tepals that overlap; tepals can recurve and twist; the tepals are light lavender blue for two thirds of their length with a crimson tinge in the final third nearest the tip; tepals white at base; wavy margins; back of tepal is a light purple with broad white central bar; prominent stamen with white anther that fades to brown and greeny-white filament that is purple at its base; prominent off-white pistil; one observer has noted a violet scent.

Foliage Ternate. Ovate-cordate.

Special Features Suitable for container and for cutting. Award of Garden Merit, Royal Horticultural Society, UK.

PLATE 31. 'Ernest Markham'.

'ERNEST MARKHAM'

This is one of the best red clematis and for that reason is often used for hybridising. It scores for its glowing colour and abundant continuous flowering. Lovely as a cut flower.

Name After Ernest Markham of Gravetye Manor, Sussex, author, clematarian and horticulturist.

Origin Probably one of the seedlings given to Ernest Markham and William Robinson by Francisque Morel when he closed his nursery. At Gravetye Manor it was known as 'Red Seedling'. S.R. Whitehead however states it was raised by Ernest Markham in 1926. On the death of Markham in 1937 the seedling passed to Jackman of Woking which named and introduced it.

Habit Deciduous. Climber. Vigorous. Grows to 4.5m (15ft). Profuse flowerer. If not pruned starts flowering in late spring and continues until early autumn. If severely pruned gives a stronger display from mid-summer. Likes sun.

Flower Upright open flower up to 15cm (6in); 6-8 tepals that overlap at base; tepals may recurve inwards and twist at tips; textured; tepals are a glowing velvety red with lighter colour at centre of tepal; wavy edge; back of tepal is pinky-white with paler stripe at centre; anther mauve turning brown; filament white with violet tinge at base; pistil off-white; firm stalk.

Foliage 5 leaflets, light green, entire.

Special Features Award of Garden Merit, Royal Horticultural Society.

PLATE 32. 'Lady Betty Balfour'.

'LADY BETTY BALFOUR'

This is a large lovely velvety flower that appears unexpectedly in late summer and flowers into the autumn. Dark tepals contrast with light centre. Its lateness extends the flowering period of the viticellas. It is beautiful in flower arrangements.

Name After a client of Jackman of Woking.

Origin Raised by Jackman of Woking, and introduced in 1910. Parentage said to be 'Gipsy Queen' x 'Beauty of Worcester'.

Habit Deciduous. Climber. Vigorous. Grows to 4.5m (15ft). Flowers very late – late summer to mid-autumn – so place in a sunny position.

Flower Upright open flower up to 12cm (4½in); 6 velvety overlapping tepals; deep purple tepals, white at base; wavy margins; at back central white bar; prominent stamens with light-yellow anther and white filament; pistil off-white; firm stalks.

Foliage Ternate.

Special Features Very late flowering. Good for cutting.

PLATE 33. 'Mrs Spencer Castle'.

'MRS SPENCER CASTLE'

A desirable clematis for its lovely clear colouring in a semi-double flower. Autumn crop, more abundant, are single flowers and equally attractive. Excellent flower for cutting.

Name After person unknown.

Origin Raised by Jackman of Woking and introduced by them in 1913.

Habit Deciduous. Climber. Fairly vigorous. Grows to 2m (6ft). Flowers as a semi-double in early summer and later with single blooms. East, south and west aspects.

Flower 6 tepals that overlap at base; tepals are pinky-violet tinged with rosy-red at centre of tepal towards the base; on back of tepal rosy-violet bar; anther light-yellow; filament rosy-violet; pistil off-white; long firm stalks.

Foliage Ternate. Mid-green.

Special Features Useful for cutting.

PLATE 34. 'Perle d'Azur'.

PLATE 35. 'Voluceau'.

'PERLE D'AZUR' (Plate 34, top left)

A plant for every garden. The world's most popular clematis. Very vigorous. Takes after its viticella parent. Specially appeals for its light colour – uncommon in clematis. So vigorous that its raiser compared it to a montana. If spread out makes a very wide plant. Very effective climbing over a wall to the other side, which hides its barren legs. Makes a fine cut flower.

Usually free of wilt when mature, but has been known to succumb when a young plant. If this occurs cut to the ground. It will quickly make new growth. Nothing should deter you from growing this plant.

Name Meaning azure pearl.

Origin Raised by Francisque Morel of Lyon-Vaise, France, in 1885. *C. lanuginosa* 'Coerulea' x *C. viticella* 'Modesta'.

Habit Deciduous. Climber. Very vigorous. When introduced described as of 'vigueur extraordinaire' and compared to a montana. Grows to 5m (16ft). Flowers early summer to early autumn. Any aspect.

Flower Horizontal open flower to 15cm (6in); 6 tepals with no overlap may recurve at tip giving flower a round appearance; tepals are deep violet with stronger colour in centre and this may have a red tinge; back is paler violet and white at centre; three central dark violet ridges tinged with red at base; anther yellow; filament green; prominent off-white pistil; long stalks; flowers in cymes.

Foliage Large. 3-5 leaflets. Mid-green.

Special Features Award of Garden Merit. Royal Horticultural Society. Makes a cut flower.

'VOLUCEAU' (Plate 35, bottom left)

This is a neglected beauty that is worthy of more attention. Blooms are large, red, and velvety. It keeps coming with series after series of blooms. One of the best of all red clematis.

Name Meaning - after a person.

Origin Raised by A. Girault of Orléans, France, in 1970. 'Ville de Lyon' x 'Pourpre Mat'.

Habit Deciduous. Climber. Vigorous. Grows to 3.6m (12ft). Continuous blooming. Profuse flowering. Flowers mid-summer to mid-autumn. Any aspect.

Flower Upright open flower up to 18cm (7in); 6 tepals that do not overlap but may recurve and twist; colour is dark reddy purple with lighter bar in centre; dark violet at base of tepal; velvety surface; back of tepal – pinky-silver fades pleasantly; long stalks; very prominent stamen; anther yellow; filament white tinged with violet; prominent off-white pistil.

Foliage Ternate.

Special Features Makes good flower for cutting.

PLATE 36. *C. viticella* 'Joan Baker' is a promising new introduction. From the UK.

CHAPTER FOUR
Supplementary List of Viticellas

In earlier chapters viticellas that are available to the gardener have been described. If they are not in general circulation the gardener can only have an academic interest in them, however worthy they may be. Yet there are indeed excellent viticellas not so readily available, and these are listed here. In this section very new viticellas not yet commercially listed are also included. In addition, known plants appear which are not regarded as garden worthy though of interest to the keen collector. To be listed here tells nothing of a viticella's merit; a number of new entrants to the garden are likely to come from this list.

As viticellas are vigorous and readily make seed it is inevitable that many seedlings will be produced. However, for a viticella to be garden worthy it must be shown to be distinctive from existing plants.

Viticellas are available in eleven countries and the countries of availability are listed alphabetically.

PLATE 37. *C. viticella* 'Kasmu' from Estonia.

PLATE 38. *C. viticella* 'Romantika' from Estonia.

ESTONIA

All the clematis below were bred by Uno and Aili Kivistik, Tallinn, Estonia and the list has been prepared with their assistance. In addition there has been consultation of the catalogue of G. Toovere.

'AINO' (Feminine name)

Light lavender blue flowers with a pink stripe. Yellow stamens. Flowering season from July till September. Flower diameter 12cm (4¾in). 6 tepals. Height up to 1.5-2m (5-6½ft). Introduced in 1981 by crossbreeding 'Ville de Lyon' and mixed pollen.

'EETIKA' (Ethics)

Pale red flowers. Purple stamens. Flowers at the end of June and July. Flower diameter 12cm (4¾in). 4-6 tepals. Height up to 1.5m (5ft). Introduced in 1984 by crossbreeding 'Hagley Hybrid' and 'Jubileinyi-70'.

'ENTEL'

Pink tepals. Introduced in 1984. 4-6 tepals. Flowers early to late summer. Flower 8-10cm (3¼-4in) across. Height up to 3m (10ft). Introduced in 1984 by cross-breeding 'Hagley Hybrid' and *C. viticella* 'Alba Luxurians'.

'JUULI' (July)

C. integrifolia x *C. viticella*. Height to 1.5m (5ft). Blue. Conspicuous white stamens. 10-12cm (4-4½in) across. Scented. Non climbing. Similar habit to 'Hendersonii'. Introduced in 1985.

'KAARU'

Flowers early summer to early autumn. 4-6 tepals. 11-13cm (4-5in) across bloom. Climbs to 2.5m (8ft). Rich dark red blossom. Introduced in 1984. 'Hagley Hybrid' by mixed pollen.

PLATE 39. *C. viticella* 'Viola' from Estonia.

'KASMU' (syn. 'Signe') (Seaside town in Estonia)
Attractive crêpe-like surface. Blooms up to 12cm (4½in) across. 4-6 tepals. Deep violet colour to tepals and cream anthers. Height to 2.5m (8ft). Likely to rival 'Emilia Plater' and 'Prince Charles'. Introduced in 1987 (Plate 37).

'KIEV' (Capital city of the Ukraine)
Dark purple. 6 tepals. Yellow stamens with purple tips. Flowers midsummer to early autumn. Flowers 12-14cm (5-5½in) across and on long stems. Height up to 3m (10ft).

'KOMMEREI'
Bordeaux-red flowers. Purple stamens. Flower diameter 14cm (5½in). 6 tepals. Height up to 3m (10ft). Introduced in 1985 by crossbreeding 'Hagley Hybrid' and 'Jubileinyi-70'. Abundant flowerer.

'MIIKLA' (Riddle)
Pinkish flowers with a white stripe. Deep purple stamens. Flowering season from July till September. Flower diameter 13cm (5in). 6 tepals. Height up to 2m (7ft). Prune hard. Introduced by Uno and Aili Kivistik in 1982 by crossbreeding 'Ville de Lyon' and mixed pollen. Abundant flowerer.

'MIKELITE' (Feminine name)
Dark purple. Yellow stamens. Introduced in 1987. From 'Mme Julia Correvon'. Height to 3m (10ft). 4-6 tepals. Flower diameter up to 14cm (5½in). Useful low plant to clamber over shrubs. Useful for container.

'MU-MERI' (My sea)
6 tepals, 12-14cm (4½-5½in) diameter. Grows to 2m (6ft). Violet blue tepals and yellow stamens. Introduced in 1981. 'Ville de Lyon' x pollen mixture.

'PIRKO' (Feminine name)
Lavender-pink striped flowers with yellow stamens. Introduced in 1987. Height up to 2.5m (8ft). 6 tepals. Diameter of flower up to 12cm (4in).

'RIISTIMAEGI' (After range of mountains)
Lavender-blue flowers with a red stripe. Yellowish pink stamens. Flowers at the end of June and in July. Flower diameter 12-14cm (4½-5in). 6 tepals. Height up to 1.5m (5ft). Bred in 1982 by crossbreeding 'Ernest Markham' and mixed pollen. Abundant flowerer.

'ROMANTIKA' (Romance)

Dark violet flowers. Greenish yellow stamens. Flowering season from the end of June till September. Flower diameter 13cm (5in). 4-6 tepals. Height up to 2.5m (8ft). Prune hard. Bred in 1983 by crossbreeding 'Devjatyj Val' and mixed pollen. Abundant flowerer. One of the best Estonian clematis (Plate 38). Awarded Certificate of Merit, British Clematis Society, 1998.

'TARTU' (An Estonian university town by that name)

Introduced in 1983. Light violet tepals and yellow stamens. Height up to 2m (6½ft). 4-6 tepals. Diameter to 18cm (7in). 'Devjatyj Val' with mixed pollen.

'TEKSA' (Jeans)

Light lavender-blue flowers with white spots. Light brown stamens. Flowering season from mid-July till September. Flower diameter 13cm (5in). 6 tepals. Height up to 2m (6½ft). Introduced in 1981 by crossbreeding 'Ernest Markham' and mixed pollen. Abundant flowerer.

'TENTEL'

Pink flowers. Greenish yellow stamens. Flowering season from July till September. Flower diameter 10-11cm (4-4¼in). 6 tepals. Height up to 3m (10ft). Prune hard. Introduced in 1984 by crossbreeding 'Jubilejnyj 70' and mixed pollen. Abundant flowerer.

'TRIINU' (Feminine name)

Reddish-pink flowers with a red stripe. Brown stamens. Flowering season from July till September. Flower diameter 13cm (5in). 6 tepals. Height up to 3m (10ft). Introduced in 1982 by crossbreeding 'Ville de Lyon' and mixed pollen.

'TRIKATREI'

Dark violet flowers. Greenish-brown stamens. Flowering season from July till September. Flower diameter 9-11cm (3½-4in). 4-6 tepals. Height up to 3m (10ft). Introduced in 1984 by crossbreeding 'Jubileinyi-70' and mixed pollen'. Abundant flowerer.

'UHTSI'

Bluish-violet flower. 4-6 tepals. Up to 11cm (4½in) across. Height to 2.2m (7ft). Introduced in 1984. 'Madam Bajun' crossed with a viticella.

'VIOLA' (Feminine name)

Bluish violet flowers. Greenish yellow stamens (Plate 39). Flowering season from July till September. Flower diameter 15cm (6in). 6 tepals. Height up to 2.5m (8ft). Introduced in 1983 by crossbreeding 'Lord Nevill' and mixed pollen. Abundant flowerer (Plate 39).

PLATE 40. *C. viticella* 'Madame Grangé'. From France.

FRANCE

'MADAME GRANGÉ' (syn. *C. lanuginosa* 'Purpurea')
Raised by M. Théophile Grangé of Orléans, France, and introduced in 1877. Large Flowered viticella. Dark rich maroon-purple tepals and beige stamens. Foliage 3-5 leaflets. Flowers mid-summer to early autumn. Flower up to 12cm (4½in); tends to fade badly (Plate 40).

GERMANY

'ALBIFLORA'
Clear white flowers. Medium-sized flowers. May be found wild in same location as the type.

'ROSEA'
Blooms mid-summer to mid-autumn. Blooms 2-3cm (¾-1¼in) across. Grows to 2.4m (8ft). Dainty clear rose and rich blossom. Globe-shaped.

'PURPUREA PLENA'
Dull grey-purple flower. Double. 5cm (2in) across bloom. Bred by Morel originally.

HOLLAND

'CICCIOLINA'
Raised and introduced by Hans Vermeulen, Holland, in 1996, as a seedling of 'Minuet'. Name refers to the Italian star 'La Cicciolina'. Flower: small. Tepals: pale purple with white middle. Stamens: cream.

'LE PETIT PRINCE'
Raised and introduced by Hans Vermeulen, Holland, in 1996. Name refers to his son Floor and the book by Antoine de Saint-Exupéry. Flower: small, purple, and irregular in shape.

PLATE 41. *C. viticella* 'Walenburg'. From Holland.

'SMALL PURPLE'

Raised and introduced by Pieter Zwijnenburg Jr, Boskoop, Holland, around 1994. Flower: small and purple coloured.

'WALENBURG'

Chance seedling discovered in the garden of the Walenburg Estate, by D.M. van Gelderen, Esveld Nurseries, Boskoop, Holland. Introduced around 1990. Tepals: margin bright (clear) purple; middle-white with purple veins; base white; outside also purple coloured. Stamens: filaments green, anthers with purple tip. Pistil: style and stigma purple. Similar to 'Minuet' but flower larger and brighter coloured (Plate 41).

The above group has been prepared with the assistance of Wim Snoeijer, and are all listed in that invaluable work of reference: Snoeijer, W. (1996) *Checklist of Clematis Grown in Holland.*

PLATE 42. *C. viticella* 'Black Prince'. From New Zealand.

LATVIA

'JEANNE'
Introduced by Janis Replens.

'PAVASARIS'
Introduced by Janis Replens.

'VEEJINJSH' (Breeze)
Introduced 1985 by Janis Replens. Red-purple. 8-10cm (3½-4in) diameter. Greenish-yellow anthers. Seedling of 'Madame Julia Correvon'. More prolific than parent. Hardy.

NEW ZEALAND

'BLACK PRINCE'
Recent introduction raised by Alistair Keay of Christchurch, New Zealand. 4 tepals are reddy black at first opening with lighter central stripe. Nodding bells at first. Height up to 3m (10ft). Flower has satiny texture. Tepals silver outside. Deep purple anthers and green filaments. Blooms in cymes, are 7cms (2½in.) across (Plate 42).

POLAND

The clematis below were raised by Brother Stefan Franczak from free pollination and the list was prepared with his assistance.

'DOMINIKA' (Feminine name)
Pale blue tepals. Creamy-white stamens. Flower of 13cm (5in) diameter. Height 2m (6½ft) (Plate 43).

'KAROLINA KOZKA' (Heroine of World War I)
Proclaimed blessed by Pope John Paul II in 1978). Lilac-rose tepals with lilac- rose stamens. Flowers to 20cm (8in) across. Flowering early to late summer. Any aspect. Height to 1.8m (6ft) (Plate 44).

'OLENKA' (Feminine name)
Tepals are bronze-lilac in colour. Cream stamens. Flower 11cm (4in) across.

'SLOWIK'
Violet tepals. Creamy stamens. Flower is 9-13cm (4-5in) across. Strong grower. Height to 3.5m (12ft).

'SOLINA' (Place in southern Poland)
Tepals are lilac in colour. Flower 9-15cm (3½-6in) across. Abundant flowerer.

'SYLWIA' (Feminine name)
Blue-violet tepals. Coffee-coloured stamens. Flower is 15cm (6in) across. Enjoys light shade. Abundant flowerer. Height to 3m (10ft).

SWEDEN

'BETTY'
Recent introduction by Magnus Johnson. Red-purple with white centre.

'CARMENCITA'
Raised by Magnus Johnson in 1952. Seedling of *C. viticella* 'Grandiflora Sanguinea'. Name – 'carmine colour of flower reminiscent of dark-eyed Spanish beauties'. Flowers 6-10cm (2½-4in) across. 4-6 tepals. Dark purple anthers and green filaments. Carpels are also dark purple. Flowers midsummer to early autumn. Grows to 3m (10ft) or more. Already popular in northern Europe (Plate 45).

'DOGGY'
Raised by Magnus Johnson. Flowers early summer to mid-autumn. Flower 3-4cm (1¼-1½in) across. Reddy-purple with bright centre. Resembles 'Minuet'.

'HAGELBY WHITE' (*C. campaniflora* x *C. viticella*)
Found in Hagelby Park, Stockholm, Sweden and introduced in 1998 to mark ten years of the Swedish Clematis Society. Profuse flowerer.

'HAGELBY PINK'

'HAGELBY BLUE'

'IMPY'
Recent introduction by Magnus Johnson. Purple with pale centre.

Clematis **'Cylindrica Nana'**
Raised by Magnus Johnson in 1970. About 30cm (12in) high.

'RONNY'
Recent introduction by Magnus Johnson. Red-purple with pale centre.

UKRAINE

Bred at Nikitsky State Botanic Garden, Yalta, Crimea and Botanic Gardens Kiev, Ukraine. This list has been prepared with the assistance of Professor M.A. Beskaravainaja, Voronezh, Russia.

'AI-NOR' (Heroine of novel *Waters of Naryn* by N.Z. Biryukov)
Flower 10-14cm (4-4½in); 5-6 tepals, pink tepals which are violet-blue at base; yellow stamens. Grows to 2.5m (8ft).
Introduced by M.A. Beskaravainaja at Yalta. 1972. 'Ville de Lyon' x *C. lanuginosa* 'Candida'.

PLATE 43. *C. viticella* 'Dominika'. From Poland.   PLATE 44. *C. viticella* 'Karolina Kozka'. From Poland.

'ALEXSANDRIT' (For a semi- precious stone)
>   Raspberry-coloured flowers which bleach slightly. Yellow stamens. Flowering
>   season from July till September. Flower diameter 12-14cm (4½-5½in).
>   6 tepals. Height up to 3m (10ft). Introduced in 1967 at Yalta by M.A.
>   Beskaravainaja by crossbreeding 'Ville de Lyon' and *C. lanuginosa* 'Candida'.

'AZHURNYI'
>   Flower 10-12cm (4-4¼in). 6 tepals. Purple-violet. Grows to 2.5m (8ft). A
>   cross of 'Nelly Moser'and 'Kermesina'. Bred by M. Orlov, Kiev, 1965.

'GNOM'
>   Flower to 6cm (3in). 4-6 tepals. Purple colour. Height to 2m (6ft). A cross
>   between 'Ville de Lyon' and 'Kermesina'. Bred by M. Orlov in Kiev, 1970.

PLATE 45. *C. viticella* 'Carmencita'. From Sweden.

PLATE 46. *C. viticella* 'Foxtrot'. From the UK.

'JADVIGA VALENSIS' (Named after breeder's mother)
Flower is 11-16cm (4½-6in) in diameter. 6 tepals are greenish pink at first and turn white. Stamens light yellow. Raised in 1961 at Yalta by A. N. Volosenko-Valensis. 'Ville de Lyon' x *C. lanuginosa* 'Candida'.

'LESNAJA OPERA' (Forest Opera)
Introduced by M.A. Beskaravainaja at Yalta in 1972. Shrubby liane 2.5-3m (80-10ft) high. Leaves trifoliate. Florets are open 10-14cm (4-5½in) in diameter. 5-6 tepals; rounded lilac-white. Anthers yellow. Flowers from July until September.

PLATE 47. *C. viticella* 'Burford Princess'. From the UK.

PLATE 48. *C. viticella* 'Joan Baker'. From the UK.

'MASKARAD' (Masquerade)

'NEGRITJANKA' (African Girl)

Deep purple flowers. Reddish-purple stamens (Plate 50). Flowering season from July till September. Flower diameter 10-12cm (4-4½in). 6 tepals. Height up to 3m (10ft). Bred in 1964 by M. Orlov in Kiev by crossbreeding 'Gipsy Queen' and *C. viticella*. Becoming available in Europe (Plate 50).

'NIKITSKIJ ROZOVYJ' (After a person)

6 tepals. Diameter of 12-14cm (4½-5½in); bright pink; grows to 3m (10ft). Yellow stamens. Introduced by A.N. Volosenko-Valensis and M.A. Beskaravainaja at Yalta in 1965. 'Ville de Lyon' x *C. lanuginosa* 'Candida'.

'RASSVET' (The dawn)

6-8 tepals. Diameter of 14-18cm (5½-7in); white or whitish-pink; grows to 3.m (10ft). Yellow stamens. Introduced by M.A. Beskaravainaja in 1972. 'Ville de Lyon' x *C. lanuginosa* 'Candida'.

UNITED KINGDOM

'AMETHYST PAGODA'

Title is provisional for promising seedling from 'Pagoda'. To be introduced by Treasure's of Tenbury, Tenbury, Worcs., UK. A deeper coloured 'Joan Baker'.

'BROCADE'

Raised by Barry Fretwell about 1993 at Peveril Nursery, Devon, UK. Free-flowering. Light red colour to tepals. Flower shaped as a montana.

'BURFORD PRINCESS'

Raised by Treasure's of Tenbury, U.K. in 1997. A lilac-edged 'Minuet' (Plate 47).

'DANAE'

Grey-blue striped tepals. A seedling named after the finder and introduced by Treasure's of Tenbury, Tenbury, Worcs., U.K. in 1998.

'DUCHESS OF SUTHERLAND'

Classed by some authorities as a Large Flowered viticella. 6 attractive rosy-pink tepals and bright cream stamens. By reputation said to be difficult to grow.

'ERIOSTEMON'

An alternative to 'Hendersonii'. Lobelia-blue tepals. Shorter flower than alternate. Origin unknown but probably originated from Belgium or The Netherlands about 1830 (see also pages 40 and 47).

'HEATHER HERSCHELL'
A new introduction from Barry Fretwell of Peveril Nursery, Devon, UK. Colour soft to deep pink.

'FOXTROT'
A lilac-edged 'Minuet'. Deep purple stamens. Raised by Barry Fretwell, Perveril Nursery, Devon, UK. A crinkly tepalled 'Minuet' (Plate 46).

'JOAN BAKER'
Bred by Bill Baker of Tidmarsh, near Pangbourne, UK and named after his wife. Cross of *C. viticella* and 'Etoile Rose'. The bell-shaped flower opens to a star-shaped flower, up to 6cm (2½in) long. 4 tepals attractively twist and recurve. Tepal is rosy-mauve on the inside. On the outside the tepal is rosy-mauve centrally and silver along the edge. Yellow prominent stamens. A promising newcomer (Plate 48).

'KATHERYN CHAPMAN'
Introduced by Sheila Chapman, Essex, UK, in 1998. Seedling from 'Minuet'. Lemon tepals, fading to white. Pale pink stripe behind.

'KING GEORGE V'
Has been classed by some authorities as a Large Flowered viticella. Lacks vigour of viticellas. Flesh-pink tepals with bright pink bar.

'RAYMOND EVISON' or ' Nana Raymond Evison'
A dwarf viticella from the Guernsey Clematis Nursery Ltd and to be used in hybridising. Named after the company proprietor (Plate 53).

'SHAUFORD'
A red viticella raised by Vince and Sylvia Denny of Broughton, Lancashire, UK, and named after the location where it was found in Somerset, UK.

'STURMINSTER'
Raised by Sylvia and Vince Denny of Broughton, Lancashire, UK. More purple than the blue of the type. Inside of tepal like 'Elvan' with well defined white areas at middle of tepal and base of tepal. Colours less defined on outside of tepal than 'Elvan' but more than the type. Nodding bell. Named after location where found at Sturminster, Dorset, UK (Plate 49).

'VANESSA'
Raised by Sylvia and Vince Denny of Broughton, Lancashire, UK. Introduced 1996. Named after lady member of British Clematis Society. Pale-violet and violet. Crêpey surface. Strong grower (Plate 51).

'ZINGARO' (Gipsy)
Raised and introduced by Robin Savill at Pleshey, Essex, UK, in 1998. Semi-nodding. Bright mauve pink tepal with paler bar.

PLATE 49. *C. viticella*
'Sturminster'. From the
UK.

PLATE 50. *C. viticella*
'Negritjanka'. From the
Ukraine.

UNITED STATES OF AMERICA

CLEMATIS CRISPA

This native American viticella produces a beautiful bell-shaped flower but too small a display to make it a regular garden choice outside the USA in the Standard Zone. Grows to 1.2m (4ft). Lavender-blue colour on outside of tepal. Flowers mid-summer to early autumn. Fragrant. Suitable to clamber amongst low-growing shrubs (Plate 52).

PLATE 51. *C. viticella* 'Vanessa'. A recent introduction. From the UK.

PLATE 53. *C. viticella* 'Nana Raymond Evison'. From Guernsey.

PLATE 52. *C. crispa*. From the USA.

CHAPTER FIVE
Trouble-Free Clematis
All Year Round

The reader may be surprised to know that there is a clematis in bloom every month of the year. But viticellas bloom, from approximately early summer to early autumn. The rest of the year can be filled with trouble-free plants from the other eleven groups of clematis thus extending and supplementing the colour from the flowering of the viticellas. This chapter is devoted to making suggestions so that the reader can have clematis in flower in the garden throughout the year.

The eleven groups, together with the Viticella Group, cover the year and each group will be taken in turn starting with Group I in early winter and proceeding through winter, spring, summer and autumn back to early winter with Group XII.

GROUP I The Evergreen Group

These clematis are the first to flower in early winter. Unlike the other groups they do not shed their leaves in winter and are thus evergreen. They need no pruning.

Three clematis can be recommended to cover a period from early winter to early spring.

1. *Clematis napaulensis*
   Starts flowering late autumn or early winter. In the Standard Zone it needs the protection of a conservatory. Can be grown out of doors in the Warm Zone. Cream flowers in clusters. Very attractive foliage. Makes lovely seed heads. Fragrant. Up to 3m (10ft) in height. Winter evergreen but no leaves in the summer.

2. *Clematis cirrhosa*
   Starts flowering early or mid-winter. Needs the shelter of a warm wall out of the wind in the Standard Zone. Is vigorous to 6.1m (20ft). The flowers are yellow-white hanging bells and scented (citrus). The foliage is attractive, fern-like, and may turn bronze in the winter. The four tepals may be freckled on the inside.

3. *Clematis armandii*
   Starts flowering in early spring. Hardiest of this group. Flourishes out of the wind on a sheltered wall. Makes a very wide and high plant up to 15ft (4.5m) x 15ft (4.5m). Large leathery glossy leaves. Produces clusters of creamy white flowers bell-shaped at first, and then opening almost flat. Heavily scented. Cultivars are 'Apple Blossom', white, tinged with pink, (Plate 54) and 'Snowdrift' (white), a most desirable plant when there is room for it

GROUP II The Alpina Group

They flower in early to late spring. They are compact climbers from 1.8m (6ft) to 2.75m (9ft). They are very hardy. Will grow in poor soil and can be grown on north-facing walls.

The blooms are single bells about 4-5cm (1½in). The bells are made up of four tepals which taper to a point. As the flowers mature they may open flat. Inside the flower are tepal-like stamens, staminodes (these are abortive and infertile stamens

PLATE 54. Pinky-white, sweet smelling *C. armandii* 'Apple Blossom' with *Cydonia* 'Japonica'.

placed between the fertile stamens and the tepals), which are usually of a different colour to the tepals and so add to the attractiveness of the bloom. Blooms are followed by pretty seed heads. The leaves are delicate, and usually a soft green.

This group requires no pruning. However if the growth has spread outside its allotted space, the plant can be tidied into place after it has flowered.

Two alpinas are recommended:

1. *C. alpina* 'Frances Rivis'
    Largest flower of the group. Elegant flower. Rich blue tepals and white staminodes, slightly suffused with violet.

2. *C. alpina* 'Jacqueline du Pré'
    Rosy-mauve tepals and powder pink staminodes. Large bloom (Plate 55).

PLATE 55. *Clematis alpina* 'Jacqueline du Pré' with saxifrage.

PLATE 56. *Clematis macropetala.*

GROUP III The Macropetala Group

They start blooming slightly later than the alpinas, from mid to late spring and also coincide with them. Similar to the alpinas in many respects they differ in having a layer of longer staminodes under the tepals, sometimes protruding, and thus giving an impression of a double rather than a single bell. Some would argue that this quality makes them the more attractive plants.

Like the alpinas they are compact in habit, very hardy, will grow on north-facing walls and climb up to 2.4m (8ft) and are more vigorous than alpinas. The seed heads of this group are amongst the best of all clematis. As with the alpinas no pruning is required but they can be 'tidied' after flowering.

Two macropetalas are recommended:

PLATE 57. *Clematis montana* 'Freda'.

PLATE 58. *Clematis montana* 'Mayleen'.

1. *C. macropetala*
   This is the type plant. Lavender-blue tepals and white inner staminodes. A fine plant (Plate 56).
2. *C. macropetala* 'Markham's Pink'
   Bright pink tepals and creamy-pink staminodes. The plant is covered with lovely double bells.

GROUP IV The Montana Group

These flower from late spring to early summer. They are the 'giants' of the clematis world. They are very vigorous, cover a large area and produce flowers in profusion. The most vigorous can climb to 9.1m (30ft) and beyond. Many are scented. Flowers of four tepals vary in size from 5 cm (2in) to 9cm (3½in). They need no pruning.

The montanas have some disadvantages. They flower for only three to four weeks. In a hard winter the stems are leafless twigs. Therefore they are best grown where they are not seen from the house. The colour will attract you out of doors to see them in flower. Nevertheless, for their outstanding and dramatic flowering, they are plants for every garden.

Two are recommended here:

1. 'Freda'
   For a small garden. Most attractive cherry-pink flower with deeper pink on margin and golden stamens. Fine coppery foliage (Plate 57).
2. 'Mayleen'
   For a large garden. Very vigorous and easy to grow. Large bloom with prominent boss of golden stamens. Strongly scented (Plate 58).

PLATE 59. *Clematis* x *cartmanii* 'Joe'.

GROUP V The Rockery Group

Most are in flower mid-spring to mid-summer and therefore coincide with Groups III and IV. Interest, by clematarians, has only developed in this group in recent years but alpine specialists have been interested in them for many years. The plants are short from a few centimetres to 61-91cm (2-3ft). Although suitable for rockeries these plants grow well in a border as long as they have good drainage and are well watered.

Two exceptional New Zealand plants are recommended. New Zealand clematis have separate male and female plants. The male makes the larger flower.

1. *C. marmoraria*
   The shortest clematis. A gem. A cushion of attractive leaves up to 25.5cm (10in) at most. Covered with bloom in spring creamy-white tinged with green, reminiscent of buttercups. Slow to start and may take three to four years to flower. In very cold areas may need to be grown indoors in pots and the pots put into the ground for the flowering period. The seed heads are spectacular.

2. *C.* x *cartmanii* 'Joe' and 'Joanna'
   This is a larger plant than the above and covering an area up to 61cm (2ft) square. At flowering the plant is covered with pure white or creamy-white flowers often with an attractive tinge of green. An outstanding plant (Plate 59).

GROUP VI The Early Large Flowered Clematis

These flower in late spring, early summer, and mid-summer. They can coincide with Groups IV and V. They are amongst the largest blooming and conspicuous of clematis. They flower on growth made the previous year. Thus they are only lightly pruned in early spring or flowers would be lost. Unhappily, this is a problem group which is susceptible to stem rot (clematis wilt). Thus special care and the antifungal treatment described later is required.

The clematis recommended below are not entirely free of the risk of developing stem rot but experience has shown that they are less susceptible than most in this group. The first two flower early in late spring. Three have single blooms, two have striped blooms and one has double blooms.

1. 'Lasurstern'
   Outstanding plant for its vigour, trouble-free nature and abundance of bloom. Handsome flower with rich deep mauve-blue tepals and white stamens. Second crop in late summer. Grows up to 3.6m (12ft).

2. 'Nelly Moser'
   This old favourite still has a prominent place in the garden for its attractive early flowers and vigorous habit. Tepals of pale mauve-pink with carmine bars very attractive at bud stage. Maroon stamens. To 2.5m (8ft). Second crop later. Tends to fade in strong sun and is best grown in semi-shade.

3. 'Niobe'
   Velvety ruby-red tepals and golden stamens. Almost black when it first opens. Flowers continuously. Pruning optional. Vigorous to 2.5m (8ft).

4. 'Mrs Cholmondeley'
   Lavender-blue tepals and brown stamens. Rather gappy flower. Very popular for its reliability and continuous flowering (Plate 60).

PLATE 60.
'Mrs Cholmondeley'.

PLATE 61.
'Madame Baron
Veillard' climbing into
smoke tree *(Continus
coggygria).*

5. 'Dr Ruppel'
   Rose-madder tepals with brilliant carmine bar and golden stamens. Vigorous to 3m (10ft). Profuse flowering. Very popular and probably the best striped clematis.

6. 'Proteus'
   Rose-lilac tepals and yellow stamens. Peony-like flower. Moderately vigorous to 2.5m (8ft).

GROUP VII Late Large Flowered Clematis Group
(Jackmanii Group)

These flower from mid-summer to early autumn. Their flowering can coincide with the Viticella Group. These plants flower on growth made in the year of flowering. Therefore they are severely pruned in early spring to encourage them to make a lot of growth and hence a lot of flower.

In their background there are often viticella genes. For this reason, probably, they are less susceptible to stem rot than the Early Large Flowered clematis. Stem rot can still occur. They can suffer from mildew but this is easily cured (see later).

Most grow to a good height. As they have to be pruned hard in the spring of next year anyway they can be semi-pruned in the autumn to 'tidy up' their appearance.

Five are recommended here. The first two may antedate the flowering of the Viticella Group while the fifth may postdate it.

1. 'Comtesse de Bouchaud'
   One of the finest clematis. Moderate size of bloom. Satiny-pink tepals with yellow stamens. Very free flowering up to 2.5m (8ft). Flowers early.

2. 'Hagley Hybrid'
   Probably the most reliable of all large-flowered clematis. Easy to grow. Usually resistant to stem rot. Lovely shell-pink bloom when it opens. Brown stamens. Free-flowering up to about 1.8m (6ft). Flowers early.

3. 'Madame Edouard André'
   Wine-red tepals and cream stamens. Up to 2.1m (7ft). So reliable it could be classed as a viticella.

PLATE 62. *Clematis* 'Durandii'.

4. 'Victoria'
   A neglected very fine clematis. Very reliable and good for a cold climate. Rosy-purple tepals and buff stamens. Very vigorous and free flowering to 4.8m (16ft). Its lighter flowers make it a more attractive plant than 'Gipsy Queen' and 'Jackmanii'. Makes a fine partner of either. Highly recommended.

5. 'Madame Baron Veillard'
   Very late flowering and may flower after the viticellas. Rosy-pink tepals and white stamens. Vigorous and free flowering up to 4.5m (15ft). Grow in a sunny spot as it flowers late (Plate 61).

GROUP VIII The Herbaceous Group

They flower mid-summer to early autumn, and coincide with the Viticella Group or postdate it. As the title implies this is a group of plants whose stems die down in the winter. Thus they prune themselves; a tidy-up is still recommended. They can make large plants. They are divided into two sub-sections *integrifolia* which flowers early and *heracleifolia* which flowers late. The former are tidy plants; the latter are larger and coarser. A feature of this group is that they do not use their petioles for climbing and thus they scramble and clamber. Three plants are recommended here, two *integrifolias* and one *heracleifolia*.

1. *C. integrifolia* x 'Durandii'
   Strong long-flowering plant. Has one of the finest blooms in all clematis. Indigo-blue flowers of interesting bell shape and yellow stamens. Can clamber up to 1.8m (6ft). Excellent cut flower. May antedate and coincide with the flowering of the viticellas (Plate 62).

PLATE 63. *Clematis* 'Princess Diana'.

2. *C. integrifolia* 'Rosea'
   Deep pink colour. One of the finest herbaceous plants in the garden.

3. *'Jouiniana* Praecox'
   A *heracleifolia* type. The finest scrambling and groundcover clematis. Covers a large area. Profuse production of white flowers with violet margins. Flowers obscure the coarse leaves. Will postdate the flowering of the viticellas.

(GROUP IX The Viticella Group.)
Description given in Chapters 2 and 3.

GROUP X The Texensis Group

This group contains some of the most attractive clematis flowers – upright tulips of different shades dancing in the breeze. Each hybrid has its supporters. All are attractive. Each plant makes a bush up to 2.4m (8ft). The Texensis Group can climb but enjoy scrambling and clambering over shrubs and bushes. All are so attractive that choice becomes a matter of personal preference.

1. 'Duchess of Albany'
   A clear pink with rose-pink bars. Cream stamens.

2. 'Gravetye Beauty'
   Rich ruby-red colour of tepals with red stamens.

3. 'Ladybird Johnson'
   Dusky-red colour.

4. 'Sir Trevor Lawrence'
   Crimson interior with cream stamens. Cream and red satiny mixture on the outside.

5. 'Princess Diana' (syn. 'The Princess of Wales')
   Vivid pink colour. Creamy-yellow stamens (Plate 63).

GROUP XI The Orientalis Group

They flower mid-summer to mid-autumn. This is the group of yellow clematis. They have fine foliage, a frequent bonus of spectacular seed heads and are easy to grow. The nodding flowers have attractive lantern, bell or open bell shapes. Can be pruned hard or no pruning for early flowering.

Two outstanding plants are recommended.

1. 'Bill Mackenzie'
   A fine large plant. Large open bell-shaped flower. Fine seed heads. Due to a long flowering period mid-summer to late autumn often has flowers and seed heads together. Will coincide with and postdate the flowering of the Viticella Group. The best of the group (Plate 64).

2. 'Helios'
   A very desirable introduction from Holland. Shorter plant than most in this group. Starts flowering early in late spring and may predate flowering of Viticella Group. Has long flowering period. Very productive of large light yellow flowers. Ideal over low shrubs and for a small garden.

PLATE 64. 'Bill Mackenzie'.

GROUP XII The Late Mixed Group

We have here a group of plants that flower in late summer to late autumn and not only extend the flowering period of the clematis but of the garden. Most are outstanding for a large display of bloom while some, in addition, are most fragrant. As the sun is limited in the autumn they benefit from being grown in sunny places. All can be pruned hard to control their vigour if necessary or just pruned into their allotted places. Two are recommended here.

1. *C. potaninii* var. *potaninii*
   A large plant growing up to 7.6m (25ft). The flowers have six white tepals with greenish-white stamens. With no pruning it can start flowering in early summer and goes on to late autumn. With pruning starts flowering in mid-summer.

2. *C. terniflora* (syn. *C. maximowicziana*)
   A desirable large plant up to 9.1m (30ft). It is covered with racemes of white flowers bearing a hawthorn-like scent. Needs to be in a very sunny position to flower in the Standard Zone. Can be spectacular grown outside in the Warm Zone. Can flower into late autumn, even into snow. It can companion *C. napaulensis* which by now will be flowering indoors in a conservatory. It also completes the circle of blooming through the year (Plate 65).

PLATE 65.
Clematis terniflora caught by snow.

PLATE 66. *C. viticella* 'Huldine' with rose 'Galway Bay'.

CHAPTER SIX
Cultivation of the Viticellas

Introduction

The garden care of the viticella group is easy. The plants are vigorous, predictable, and have an urge to grow. They are not sensitive, hesitant, and effete like the Early Large Flowered Group. They will almost grow without any special care but of course do better if they receive it.

They do not demand protection in the garden. Put them where you want them to make a display and they will achieve this, even in semi-shade. You can pamper them if you want some special effect.

Everything about the viticellas is easy - planting, pruning, control of diseases and propagation. They make just two demands – they must be kept well watered as they are large plants and they relish good feeding – again because they make massive growth within the course of a year.

The large flowered viticellas do need some extra care and so a special section will be devoted to their special needs.

Climatic Zones

Climate is a subject of considerable complexity. Either the subject is dealt with by a book (Jane Taylor[1] has taken this course), or it must be dealt with simply. I shall deal with it simply.

One approach is to consider climate in terms of latitude. So many other factors are involved that such an approach can be over-simple. Another approach defines climatic zones in terms of the lowest annual temperature in a territory. This approach has been worked out in the United States and produces a complex pattern that does not coincide with the pattern based on latitude. Factors additional to latitude and temperature in a territory are: 1) Height above or below sea-level; 2) the maritime status; 3) the relative pattern of oceanic currents; 4) the rainfall and snowfall; 5) the pattern of prevailing winds; 6) forestation; 7) sunshine rates; 8) direction of prevailing wind.

For an easily understood system for clematis I suggest a classification based upon three zones: Standard, Cold and Warm.

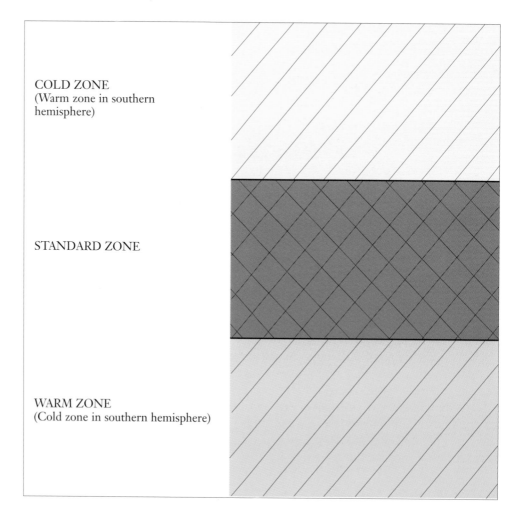

COLD ZONE
(Warm zone in southern hemisphere)

STANDARD ZONE

WARM ZONE
(Cold zone in southern hemisphere)

Figure 6. The three climatic zones of the northern hemisphere.

The Standard Zone corresponds to an area describable as mid-European and extending approximately from the Mediterranean northwards to northern Europe. The latitude is approximately from 40° to 55°. Minimum winter temperatures range from -7° to -3°C. This is an area of the most intensive cultivation of clematis. At sea level no, or only slight, protection of the plants is required in winter. The seasons are well marked in the Standard Zone. There are equivalent areas in other parts of the northern and southern hemispheres. Climatologists might loosely term this area as 'temperate'. This zone approximates to Zone V of the American classification quoted by Rehder.[2]

The Cold Zone is north, (or south in the case of the southern hemisphere), of the Standard Zone. Here plants routinely need protection from the cold in winter. Cultivation of clematis is not usually possible north of this area (or south in the southern hemisphere). Minimum winter temperatures are below -7°C.

The Warm Zone is south (or north in the case of the southern hemisphere) of the Standard Zone. Here clematis will never require protection from the cold but special measures may be required to protect the plants from heat and to guarantee a continuous supply of water. Cultivation of clematis is not usually possible as one moves south in this zone (or north in the southern hemisphere). The minimum winter temperatures in this zone are above -7°C.

Within any of these zones the gardener must still take account of the micro-climate of his garden. Growth takes place when the temperature rises over 6°C (43°F). Temperature is greatest at soil level. Temperature changes decrease with depth of soil and disappear at a depth of 1m (3ft). A soil depth of only 5cm (2in) can make a big difference in temperature. Certain clematis can be grown on a south-facing wall in the northern hemisphere but cannot be grown on a north-facing wall. Again, an east wall gets sun first and if a plant has frozen in the night, it is likely to be damaged by a thaw. Slopes facing south are warm and in a dell, out of the wind, it may be possible to grow clematis that would be damaged on an exposed site. By contrast, however, a dell with no passage of air can become a frost pocket. The height of the garden above sea-level can make a dramatic difference from similar gardens nearby not in elevated positions. Surprisingly small differences in that height make enormous differences in cultivation. The volcanic island of Madeira is a lesson in this connection: For every 100m (250ft) rise in height the temperature falls by 0.5°C (1°F).

Taking account of the zone and the micro-climate of a garden will allow most gardeners to manage effectively the cultivation of their viticella clematis.

The viticellas are the most accommodating of all the clematis groups. Originally a native of the Warm Zone, it flourishes in the Standard Zone and yet is developing a reputation of being the most useful group to grow in the Cold Zone.

REFERENCE

Taylor, Jane (1996) *Weather in the Garden*. John Murray. London.
Rehder, A (1990) *Manual of Cultivated Trees and Shrubs*. Dioscorides Press. Oregon.

PLATE 67. Long flowering *C. viticella* 'Pagoda' makes a lovely feature in a border.

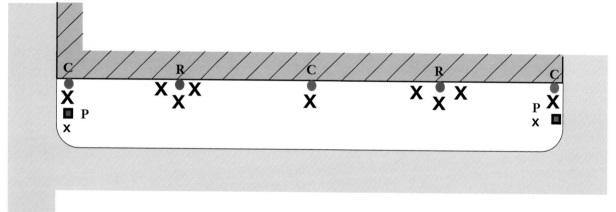

Figure 7. Planting plan for a long bed ('R' = climbing rose; 'C' = climbing shrub; 'P' = post; X = planted viticellas; x for additional viticellas).

A Garden Plan

Labels seem to have a life of their own. They break, they become indistinct and they disappear. Thus it is essential to have a plan of the garden which clearly shows the position of each viticella. This can be part of an already existing garden plan. Otherwise it can be created just for the clematis.

It is useful to divide the garden into sections giving each a name, For example 'the oval bed', 'the north bed', 'the long bed', etc. Each section can have a page of the plan to itself. A particular mark such as an 'X' can indicate the position of a viticella. Each mark bears a name of a viticella clematis.

110

PLATE 68. *C. viticella* 'Minuet' sparkles in the sun.

To make it easy, and to recognise instantly the position of a clematis, it is useful to mark on the plan permanent structures such as posts, trees, or marks on walls. The permanent structures are named on the plan. The positions of the viticella clematis are related on the plan to these permanent structures and it makes the clematis easy to find.

The plan will be invaluable in the winter when the time comes to plan new plantings for the following year. Indeed, it is possible to mark further positions for more clematis on the plan with broken crosses.

Planting

Planning

Plan your planting sometime beforehand. Consult the garden plan and decide where clematis can be planted with advantage. In the case of spring planting, time can be devoted to the planning during the winter. Indeed the holes can be prepared during the winter for spring planting. It is said that an hour's gardening in winter is as good as five hours in the summer!

The main planting of viticellas should be in the spring. At this time the soil is warming up and the plant has an urge to grow.

Choosing a Plant

There is much to be said in favour of buying a viticella from a special clematis nursery. Here the choice will be wide and expert help is available. Again, the quickest way of gaining access to many viticellas and to weigh up their merits is to visit a clematis nursery.

Viticella plants should be at least two years old. Look for a plant with more than one stem, 60-90cm (2-3ft) long. Look for good strong buds low down on the stem. See that the plant has a good root system by checking the roots are emerging through the drainage holes at the bottom of the pot. If you are in any doubt ask the nursery to display the roots to you.

Avoid one year old plants which will be found in 10cm (4in) pots and referred to in the trade as 'liners'. These are not bred for growing in the ground and if purchased should be repotted into a two-litre pot and 'grown on' for another year.

Delivery

If you order by post then your viticella will often be delivered in the autumn. There is much to be said for repotting the clematis into a larger pot, keeping it protected in a trench and well watered through the winter and planting it in the spring. It is now becoming more common for clematis nurseries to supply plants ready for planting in the spring. The main reason for wanting to supply clematis in the autumn is that nurseries do not wish to carry them through the winter. Should it not be possible to hold the plant until the spring then a container-grown clematis can be planted at any time of the year, if conditions are favourable.

Situation

Viticellas grow well in the temperate regions of the world. Ideally they enjoy growing in full sun away from the wind, but are very accommodating and will grow well in less than ideal situations. Viticellas will grow in semi-shade and on north-facing walls.

Clematis, like all plants, need good drainage. If the site is not well drained the roots will be in water. If water denies oxygen to the roots then in time the plant will suffer and die.

Soil

The ideal soil is friable, well-drained, and loamy and planting in it becomes easy because it contains all the necessary conditions for a healthy plant. In practice gardeners do not find themselves with the ideal soil and it can be either too light or too heavy. Light soil is easy to work but water slips through it very quickly and it contains little nutriment. Such a soil needs the addition of humus in the form of manure, compost, peat or peat substitutes. A heavy soil may be full of nutrients but lacks drainage. Roots require not only water and nutriment but also oxygen. Oxygen will be absent if the roots are continually in water so care must be taken to drain the holes made for planting in such a heavy, clay soil. This can be done with broken brick or rubble to a depth of 10-15cm (4-6in).

Clematis grow satisfactorily in soil which is neutral, slightly acid or slightly alkaline. The ideal pH for growing clematis is not yet known as no experimentation has taken place.

PLATE 69. *C. viticella* 'Mrs T. Lundell' makes a fine companion for rose 'Chaplin's Pink' in the Garden of the Rose, St Alban's, UK.

The Hole

This should be large enough to take the roots of the viticella comfortably without them being squeezed together. Clematis should have a hole of 45cm (18in) diameter and 60cm (2ft) deep.

When digging the hole mark out the area on the soil surface. Having removed the top layer with a spade, loosen the next layer with a fork before using the spade again to lift the soil out. Keep on loosening the soil with a fork to make your task much easier. Any soil that you discard put in the wheelbarrow and take away. (Keep good topsoil.) The commonest error is not to make the hole deep enough for clematis.

Experienced gardeners can now proceed to plant the viticella clematis like any other shrub. No special measures are required for the viticellas. In the Standard Zone unlike some clematis they do not need to be planted deeper in the soil than other plants. In the Cold Zone plant them deeper so that buds for new stems are protected from low temperatures.

For the less experienced gardener one method involving five layers will be outlined. The first, the bottom layer, is where the roots will be growing. It is known that viticella roots extend for at least 45-60cm (18-24in), even 1m (39in). Thus about 23cm (9in) is given to this layer, to give roots a good start. The roots need a rich medium for nourishment and also one which will retain water. Experts vary in their recommendations: half soil with half manure or moist, coarse, peat or with leaf mould; or half soil and half garden compost. Whatever is employed, two handfuls of bonemeal should also be added and this should be well mixed in.

The second layer should be a mere 1cm (½in) of soil or peat, and is simply a barrier to keep the roots of the viticella plant initially separate from the rich material below.

The third layer of about 23cm (9in) is where the clematis will be placed.

The fourth layer is above the clematis and extends to about 2.5cm (1in) as a blanket to the plant. The viticella plant should end up just below ground level. In the case of clematis susceptible to stem rot (wilt) the clematis end up 10cm (4in) below ground level so that extra stems can grow which will be an insurance against losing stems from stem rot. This is **not** necessary in the case of the viticellas. The only exception would be an extremely cold area where extra soil will protect the crown of the plant against unusual cold.

The material in the third and fourth layers need not be as rich as the material in the bottom area and can consist of good topsoil taken out of the hole or soil mixed with peat or leaf mould or compost. One handful of bonemeal can be added. Bonemeal should be avoided in light soils as it may attract ants and should be replaced by a general fertiliser.

The fifth layer is the lip area allowing 2cm (1in) below the soil level to make a saucer area into which water can gather either naturally or as the result of watering. Thus avoid leaving the soil convex at the top. This saucer area will also greatly facilitate the task of watering.

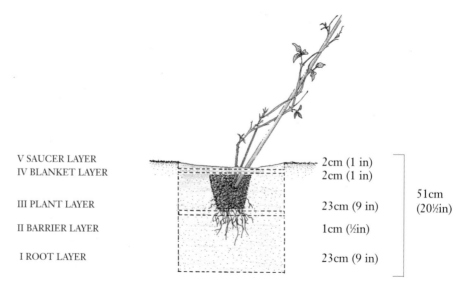

V SAUCER LAYER — 2cm (1 in)
IV BLANKET LAYER — 2cm (1 in)

III PLANT LAYER — 23cm (9 in)

II BARRIER LAYER — 1cm (½in)

I ROOT LAYER — 23cm (9 in)

51cm (20½in)

Figure 8. Five layers of planting material in a hole of 45cm (1½ft) diameter and 51cm (20½in) deep.

PLATE 70. *C. viticella*
'Venosa Violacea'
contrasts well with
C. orientalis var.
ternifolia.

Order of Planting

Plants benefit from being immersed in water for a period of about two hours before planting to ensure that the plants have not dried out.

The clematis can be extracted from its container by tapping the edge of the pot against the top of a fork stuck into the ground. A thin plastic container should be cut open with care.

First put the chosen material in the root layer (**layer one**). Cover with a thin layer of soil or peat to make the barrier layer (**layer two**). Gently spread the roots of the viticella over the surface of the barrier area. Now fill in with what you have chosen for the plant area (**layer three**), and the blanket layer (**layer four**), and leave a saucer layer at the top (**layer five**).

Firm the material around and above the plant with your foot. If a cane is not attached to the clematis, mark the planting area with a short cane or stick which will prevent the clematis from getting lost. Attach a label nearby.

Clematis should be planted at least 60cm (24in), preferably 1m (3ft), apart.

PLATE 71. In a border
viticellas 'Hendersonii'
and 'Pagoda' are on
either side of *C.
integrifolia* 'Aljonushka'.

PLATE 72. Beautiful *C. viticella* 'Elvan' embellishes any background.

Support

The stems of the clematis plant usually arrive from the nursery attached to a cane. Ensure that the stems are firmly attached to the cane and, if need be, use new ties. This cane helps support the plant during planting and can carry the stem to a wall, post, host plant or other support if long enough. After planting you can insert a new cane in the ground and tie it to the original cane to enable the plant to climb to its supporting shrub or structure.

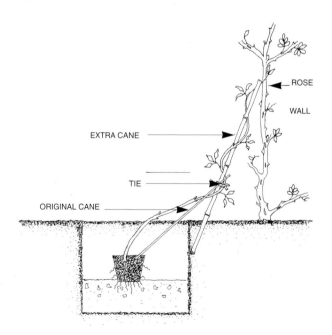

Figure 9. Original cane from a nursery can be tied to a new cane.

ROSE

WALL

EXTRA CANE

TIE

ORIGINAL CANE

116

PLATE 73. *C. viticella* 'Prince Charles' makes excellent wall cover.

PLATE 74. *C. viticella* 'Blekitny Aniol' glows at sunset.

Planting Near Walls

The soil near a wall is usually poor because rain may not reach it and the wall itself extracts water from it. Thus clematis should be planted 45cm (1½ft) or preferably 60cm (2ft) away from the wall.

There are times, however, when it is not possible to do this and the clematis has to be planted very close to the wall. This can be successfully achieved if the plant is treated as if growing in a container, in which case excavate the old poor soil and replace with new. Line the wall with slates or plastic sheeting to prevent the absorption of water. Great care must be taken to ensure that the area receives sufficient water: the equivalent of 2.5cm (1in) of water per week, that is, 10 litres (2 gallons) of water per plant per week as a minimum. In hot weather it may be necessary to give 10 litres (2 gallons) of water twice a week. Furthermore attention should be paid to ensuring that plants do not dry out during the winter for the winter rains may not reach plants close to walls.

Moving Plants

Plants should be moved from one part of the garden to another in the late autumn, winter or early spring when the soil is not frozen or waterlogged.

Winter Protection

Viticella clematis are very hardy and only need protection in exceptionally harsh conditions. Roots can be protected with a mulch of manure, bark chippings, straw, conifer prunings, crumpled paper, etc.

In very cold countries the mulch should be used after the ground has frozen to 10-15cm (3-6in). This will prevent the frozen ground from thawing and freezing deeper as it is during thawing and re-freezing that damage is done. The central area can be heaped with grit or sand and the rest covered with mulch material such as leaves, peat, straw, sawdust, to a minimum height of 10cm (4in) or ideally to 15cm (6in).

Stems can be protected with a circular layer of wire netting, or hessian sacking stuffed with leaves, or straw or bracken. Another method is to wrap the stems in a layer of horticultural fleece or polythene bubble. To protect plant stems on a wall hang a sheet of hessian sacking or fleece sheeting in front or hang netting in front of the plant and stuff it with insulating material.

Hot Climates

Being Warm Zone plants Viticellas adjust well to hot climates but protect the crowns with thick mulch or plant them under paving. Give frequent and large amounts of water and ensure there is good drainage so that water does not stay as a pool around the roots. Plant in semi-shade when possible and protect from hot winds.

Regular Inspection

Viticella plants should be visited at least once a week. There may be signs of damage or early disease and these will respond best if treated promptly. Stems of clematis may need guiding in the best direction or may need tying in. Lack of water can be immediately remedied.

PLATE 75. *C. viticella* 'Hendersonii' is a valuable long bloomer in a border.

PLATE 76. *C. viticella* 'Etoile Violette' blends happily with rose 'Compassion'.

Labelling

The ideal label shows the name clearly, is easily visible, is permanent and yet not obtrusive. It is very difficult, with any label, to achieve all these requirements. The natural elements are very strong and can do severe damage to a label even in one winter.

At the time of planting, the viticellas should be labelled but the label should not be fixed on the plant. A clematis does not like the label attached to itself, especially if it is metal. Also labels attached to plants can disappear at the time of pruning! Thus the label should be attached to either the support of the viticella or be put into the ground nearby. If the latter they can impede hoeing and may be rendered invisible by weeds. Sometimes a short wood or metal post may have to be fixed specially into the ground to support a label.

As has been said earlier there are so many hazards with labels that it is imperative to have a plan showing the position of each viticella. This plan can be consulted in the winter months and the correctness of the labels checked. Defective labels can then be put right for the growing season.

The most durable forms of labels tend to be the most expensive. The cheapest are the white or coloured plastic pieces with the name of the plant in so-called 'permanent' ink. Experience shows that a plastic piece becomes fragile after a season and the 'permanent' ink hardly visible after two seasons at most. Thus it is necessary to replace most labels every year after checking with the plan of planting. White plastic labels do not add to the beauty of the garden and should be tucked out of sight.

A Supply of Water

In theory it is possible to overwater; a hose directed continually at a piece of ground will ultimately leach all the nutrients out of it. This is unlikely to happen with the amount recommended here and in any event is likely to be counterbalanced by the rich feeding programme.

Viticella clematis require a minimum of 5 litres (1 gallon) of water a week. The importance of giving clematis sufficient water cannot be overestimated. Clematis will take up to 20 litres (4 gallons) per plant per week and in hot weather will relish 5 litres (1 gallon) per plant per day.

To be sure that you can determine exactly how much water a plant is having it is best to direct the water specifically on to the plant rather than allow it to take its share from a general garden watering.

Watering should take place out of the sun in the evenings. Water will of course be assisted by having planted your viticella correctly with a saucer area at the top of the hole. The following methods of watering can be used:

1. Watering can. It is hard work but its easy to measure the amount each plant gets.
2. By hose. If a hose is used then use a fine spray on both sides of the leaves.
3. Generalised watering. Watering by using a sprayer.
4. During planting advantage can be taken to insert a watering tube into the soil. The aim is to lead the water straight to the root area. A pipe of 12cm (4½in) diameter and 38cm (15in) long will do the job. At the bottom end of the tube there should be a few stones to allow easy drainage. An alternative watering aid is to sink an empty plant pot close to the clematis and water through this. With this system put two-thirds of the water into the pipe or pot and the rest over the soil to keep moist any roots which are near to the surface.

At the time of watering a liquid fertiliser can be given, either being dissolved into a watering can or being served from an attachment added to the hose.

The Best Watering System

The leaking, seeping or porous pipe systems are impressive and easy to install. Do a small area first and you will soon be accustomed to the fittings and method of installation. Once in place the saving of time is enormous and quickly repays the cost and effort. The pipe can be put below the surface and the water goes to the exact spot that you planned to receive it, without wastage. It is easy to control the amount of water the plants receive, but make sure that the pipe is close, within centimetres, of your viticella.

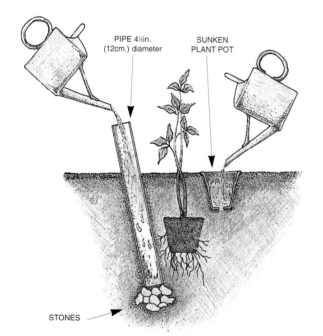

PIPE 4½in. (12cm.) diameter
SUNKEN PLANT POT
STONES

Figure 10. Plant watering is made easier by burying a plant pot or inserting a pipe.

PLATE 77. *C. viticella* 'Kermesina' hops easily over a wall.

Mulching

The main reason for using a mulch with viticellas is to retain the moisture in the ground. This is much more effective than planting the roots in the shade or planting dwarf shrubs around the plant. Dwarf shrubs compete with the clematis for water.

Additional reasons for using a mulch are that it keeps the ground cool, it suppresses weeds, it adds humus to the ground and it will also help to add nutrients to the soil.

The mulch should be applied in the spring after the soil has warmed up. Remove any dead material from the ground and burn it. Later, inorganic or liquid fertilisers can be applied through it. The fertiliser should be watered in.

Apply sufficient mulch material to cover 60 sq cm (2 sq ft) around the plant and to a thickness of at least 5-8cm (2-3in); 8-10cm (3-4in) will be even better. Do not carry the mulch material close to the stems as some of it, especially fresh manure, can damage them. Furthermore the mulch close to the crown of the clematis makes a humid situation that will encourage stem rot.

In the autumn the mulch material can be forked gently into the ground or left to protect the roots against severe weather. The following materials can be used:

1. Moist peat. This contains a little nitrogen only. It tends toward acidity and is therefore good for alkaline soils.
2. Leaf mould contains some nutrients. It is usually acid. It is excellent mulching material.
3. Farmyard manure tends to be acid. Excellent mulching material but the manure must be old and in a state when it cuts like cake.

Figure 11. The introduction of a thick layer of mulch not less than 60cm (2ft) square around the clematis is beneficial. The material used should not come into contact with the plant stems.

4. Garden compost. Tends to be acid. Excellent mulching material.
5. Well rotted straw or sawdust.
6. Grass clippings. Tends to take the nitrogen out of the soil. Should never be employed if a selected weed killer has been used on the lawn.
7. Pulverised bark. Contains few nutrients.
8. Mushroom compost. It is alkaline and therefore particularly good for acid soil. Mushroom compost has not usually been found to be satisfactory with clematis.
9. Black polythene sheeting with a hole in the sheeting from which the plant emerges. Can be disguised with bark or stones. Gives excellent results.
10. Porous sheeting which prevents weeds coming through, retains water in the soil and at the same time, being porous, allows water and fertilisers to pass easily through.
11. As a last resort stones, small brick, or shingle can also be used.

PLATE 78. *C. viticella* 'Etoile Violette' rivals *C.* 'Jackmanii' in popularity.

If materials which are liable to take nitrogen out of the soils are being used then 60-90 grams (2-3oz) of sulphate of ammonia can be spread over the ground to 1 sq m (1 sq yd) before applying the mulch.

If clematis are planted in holes in stone material, as for example on a patio, then they will flourish exceedingly because the stonework acts as a mulch. Naturally the soil in the hole must be well supplied with humus, nutrients, and water.

Feeding

In a good loamy soil little or no fertilising will be necessary but many soils do need feeding. Viticellas are very undemanding but still benefit from good nutrition.

Manure and garden compost give invaluable humus to the soil, improve drainage and the retention of water.

Most energy must be given to the plants, however, in the form of fertilisers. These should be used according to recommended strength and spread evenly and uniformly about the plant and moved gently into the soil by fork or hand or hoe.

Peat, although it contains no nourishment, is a good mulch and a soil conditioner; if used, it should be strengthened by containing an artificial fertiliser.

It is most important to ensure that manure, compost and artificial compost are spread well away from the stems of the plant – to a distance of 10cm (4in). Most of the roots are spread widely below and the fertiliser will reach them better away from the stem. Another important reason is that young manure and artificial fertiliser will rot the stems and even kill a plant.

Foliar feeding may be time-consuming but used once a week at recommended strength it is an excellent way of boosting your choice viticella plants. Its especially helpful with young clematis. It is usually possible to undertake the foliar feeding with the watering programme.

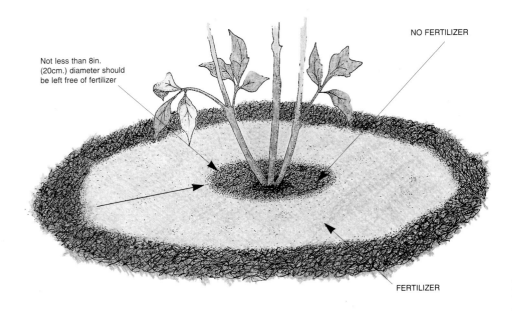

NO FERTILIZER

Not less than 8in. (20cm.) diameter should be left free of fertilizer

FERTILIZER

Figure 12. Keep artificial fertilizers away from viticella stems.

PLATE 79. Each bloom of
C. viticella 'Betty Corning'
is a gem.

Suggested Feeding Schedule

IN THE AUTUMN
1. Apply bonemeal at the rate of 100 grams (3½ oz) per sq m (per sq yd). Bonemeal is a slow-release fertiliser and will be still at work in the following spring and longer. It tends to make the ground alkaline. It is rich with phosphates and encourages root growth. It should be worked gently into the ground. In light ground bonemeal may attract ants and should be replaced by a general fertiliser.
2. Provide a mulch of garden compost or well rotted manure, spreading it to about 60cm (2ft) around the plant. The manure must be well rotted.

IN THE SPRING
1. Gently dig in the autumn manure.
2. Employ a handful of potash or artificial fertiliser rich in potash. Water it into the soil.
3. Now apply another mulch of suitable material.
4. If strong plants are required for a special reason, apply a liquid fertiliser rich in potash once a week. A well established plant will enjoy the benefit of liquid feed twice a week. Never apply the fertiliser stronger than stated in the instructions; 'little and often' is the secret to success. Water first if the soil is dry. Stop the liquid fertiliser when the viticella is in flower or it will shorten the flowering period.

IN MID-SUMMER
Give another handful of potash or a fertiliser rich in potash. Water it in.

PLATE 80. Strong *C. viticella* 'Jenny Caddick' can cope easily with holly.

Pruning

Pruning viticella clematis is simple and easy. In early spring prune last year's stems of the viticellas down to the ground. Nothing of the old stems is left above ground. New green stems appearing from the ground are left untouched (Figure 13).

It has been customary to prune viticellas down to strong shoots appearing from the old stems about 15-30cm (6-12in) from the ground. This method is out of date,

CUTS

NEW SHOOTS

Figure 13. Prune last year's stalks of viticellas at ground level allowing new green shoots to appear from the ground.

125

unnecessary, and confusing to the novice.

Do not start pruning too early in the spring. Wait for the risk of frost to disappear. During frost the old stems will help to protect the new ones from frost. Viticellas flower late in the season and once the ground warms up they have plenty of time to grow into flowering plants.

Extra Points on Pruning

1. If you are of a cautious nature, prune old stems to 15cm (6in) from the soil. Wait for green stems to appear from the ground, then prune the old stems right to the soil surface.

2. Use secateurs or scissors depending on the toughness of the shoots.

3. Always burn shoots at once after pruning. This will reduce the risk of leaving spores of fungi around.

4. Hand prune in the autumn if they look unsightly, they will come to no harm. Prune to 60-90cm (2-3ft) from the ground and if the shoots are tied together they will be unobtrusive. It is wise not to prune to the ground then as the remaining stems will protect the crown of the plant through the winter.

5. Occasionally you will need a clematis to grow to an unusual height, perhaps to get over a wall or shrub, to climb high on a pergola. The viticellas are good for this. Over two to three years prune 90-110cm (3-4ft) from the ground, not right down to the ground. The low stems will soon become brown and hard and put out green shoots from the tops of which the flowers will appear. You have now raised ground level by 90-110cm (3-4ft) which will assist the viticella in its climb. In future always prune the green shoots above the level of the brown shoots.

6. Pruning can be used to extend the flowering period by two techniques:

a) Prune only half your viticella plant. The unpruned part will flower early and so extend the period of flowering. Next year prune that half and leave unpruned the half you pruned this year.

b) Some viticellas flower early. Once the show of flowering is coming to an end prune off the upper parts of the stems which bear the flowers. The plant will often produce new shoots and they will flower late in the season and so extend the period of flowering into the autumn.

7. In the Cold Zone the plan above may need adjustment. Prune to the ground in mid-autumn after the ground has become frozen to 10-15cm (3-6in). (Avoid doing it too early or new shoots will appear and be killed by frost.) After the pruning, cover the area of the plant with thick protective material so as to prevent premature thawing and deeper freezing. The protective material is removed in mid or late spring when frosts are unlikely.

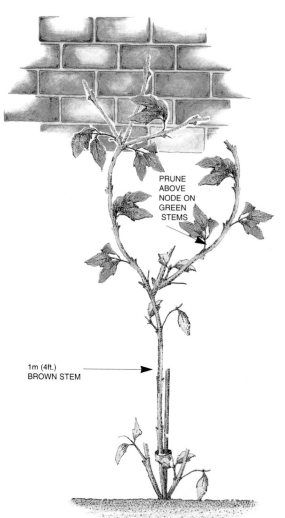

PRUNE ABOVE NODE ON GREEN STEMS

1m (4ft.) BROWN STEM

Figure 14. Helping viticellas gain height. Prune stalk 1m (4ft) from ground. Green stems will appear at this new level. Prune these green stems every year and not the brown stem. Prune green stems above a node.

PLATE 81. The cutting on the right has mildew on its leaves, stem and bud.

Diseases and Pests

Viticella clematis are remarkably healthy and suffer from no major disease particular to them. The large viticella clematis are occasionally vulnerable to stem rot. The management of 'stem rot' will be discussed later (pages 134-136).

Mildew

This tends to occur late in the season. The leaves and flowers look dusted with a grey-white powder which disfigures them but does not kill the plant. 'Etoile Rose' is the viticella most likely to be affected.

As soon as the mildew is seen apply systemic fungicides, which are very effective. Many fungicides are available against mildew. Mix at the maximum strength recommended by the manufacturers. After a thorough watering of the plant, pour the mixture, if systemic, into the root area of the viticella. This is quicker, easier and as effective as spraying. Repeat every ten days twice more. A systemic fungicide once absorbed through the roots spreads throughout the plant.

Protect 'Etoile Rose' by applying fungicide just before the plant flowers and every week thereafter until flowering has ceased.

PLATE 82. *C. viticella* 'Etoile Rose', here climbing on a wall, is susceptible to mildew.

Pests

Populations of *earwigs* build up towards late summer and attack the foliage, buds and flowers of clematis, distorting all. The earwigs can be captured by inverting pots on canes and dropped into a salty water solution or the plants dusted with Gamma HCH (Lindane) powder.

Slugs and snails attack new shoots particularly and can do great damage. Slug bait is partially successful. Also spray hiding places with liquid killer. It is said that to mulch beds with forest bark encourages a beetle to live in the bark and the beetle eats both the eggs and young snails and slugs.

Vine weevil grubs can attack the roots of clematis plants held in pots in greenhouses. Carefully inspect the clematis once removed from the pot. If any grubs are seen they should be destroyed immediately. If there are signs of extensive damage to roots then the clematis plant should be discarded.

Rabbits and pheasants in rural areas can cause massive damage to the young shoots of clematis. Plants may need to be protected by wire enclosures.

PLATE 83. The caterpillars of the vine weevil make holes in the leaf margins.

Propagation

Commercially, viticella clematis are no longer propagated by grafting but by soft wood cuttings. The gardener does not usually need a large number, but anyone who wants detailed information will find it in the companion volume *The Rose and the Clematis as Good Companions*.

The amateur can use the following methods for small numbers of extra plants, which are discussed below.

PLATE 84. Viticellas 'Prince Charles' and 'Abundance' combine to make a brilliant display on a wall.

Layering

This is the best method for producing a small number of viticella plants. The advantages are:

    a) The new plant comes true to type with the offspring having the identical characteristics of the parent.

    b) It can extend an existing plant on one or both sides which makes a larger impact. Furthermore, there will be replacement plants should the original plant die.

    c) The layered plant can be used elsewhere in the garden.

Layering can begin as soon as the ground gets warm in early spring. Some stems can be left unpruned at this time and these can be brought down to ground level and used for propagation. Layering can be done at any time until the autumn; but in this event the plants may not be ready until the following year. Spring-layered plants will have formed roots by the autumn and will be ready for 'potting up'.

Many of the viticellas grow so strong that it is possible to use a simple method. Just bring a clematis stem down to the ground, make a trench 10-15cm (4-6in) deep with your hand or trowel, gently lay the stem in the trench, twist the bark at a node, place the soil over it, place a brick over each node, and fix the end of the stem to a cane. Keep the stem well watered. Using a simple method like this probably means you will attempt to layer more clematis.

A more exact method is as follows:

a)   A long stem is gently brought down towards the ground. Old material, and not green material, is best for layering.

b)   Carefully inspect the stem to see where there are good nodes. With a sharp knife, cut below a node joint, slicing upwards about half-way through the stem to make a short 'tongue'. To keep the 'tongue' open slip a match or pebble in the elbow.

c)   Powder the cut with hormone rooting powder.

d)   With a trowel make a trench 10-15cm (4-6in) deep. In the trench place peat and soil or potting compost and soil or sharp sand. Gently peg the node down in this mixture using a piece of wire bent into the shape of a hairpin. Cover the node with the mixture.

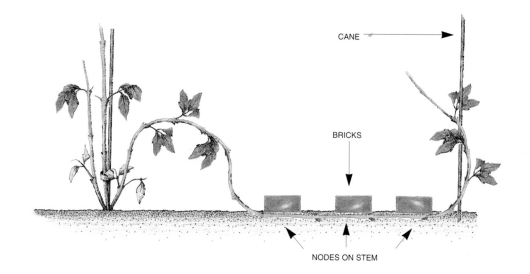

Figure 15. Simple layering of viticellas.

e) Cover the node with a good mulch, a brick, or stones to keep the area moist.

f) Mark the end of the stem with a short cane to remind you where the layer is and to fix the stem.

g) Water freely and keep watered.

h) Leave for six to 12 months. To test whether you have roots, gently pull the end of the stem; if there is resistance you have roots.

i) With secateurs, sever the layered plant from the parent plant, gently lift with fork and pot up immediately. Do not let the roots dry out. Water the pot. Feed it with liquid fertiliser. When the plant is strong it can be planted out.

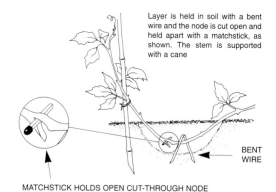

Layer is held in soil with a bent wire and the node is cut open and held apart with a matchstick, as shown. The stem is supported with a cane

BENT WIRE

MATCHSTICK HOLDS OPEN CUT-THROUGH NODE

Figure 16. Layering viticellas.

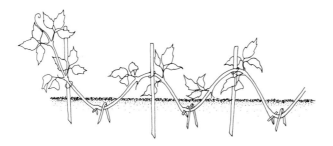

Figure 17. Serpentine layering.

Serpentine layering

Serpentine layering involves taking a particularly long shoot and a number of nodes. Each of the nodes is treated as above in the ground or in pots in the ground. Part of the stem between nodes is above ground.

Instead of putting the node into a trench it can be laid gently into a mixture in a 25cm (10in) pot. The mixture can be either soil-based potting compost, peat and soil, or compost and soil.

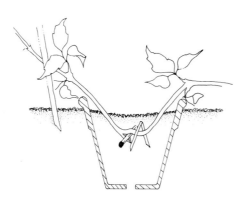

Figure 18. Layering into a pot

Division

This should be undertaken in early spring. It can be applied to a viticella once the plant is well established with a broad root area. The stems are pruned to the ground. The whole plant is carefully lifted and divided into two or more pieces. The division should be done by a sharp knife, spade, or fork (Figure 19). The pieces of plant are put straight back into the ground prepared for clematis or if they are small, planted in pots and later, when they are large enough, planted outside.

Figure 19. Plant division. Two hand forks will help to pull roots apart.

PLATE 85. *C viticella* 'Royal Velours' stands out well against a light background.

Nibbling

Nibbling is different from root division. In nibbling the parent plant remains in the ground. Careful observation reveals, especially in established plants, that the spread of the viticella is so wide that it should be possible to nibble at it and take a piece away. You may even see an extension close to an established plant. Sometimes an established plant is so broad that it is possible to nibble away at two or three corners of it. The golden rule of nibbling is that one must never risk damaging the parent plant.

The roots of clematis go very deep, and therefore a sharp spade must be placed between the parent plant and the portion to be nibbled, with the spade driven deep into the ground separating the roots of the nibbled portion from that of the main plant. The spade is then withdrawn and driven in again in three places to complete a square around the portion to be nibbled.

By pushing the spade in on the side which is most convenient, the nibbled part is then taken out of the ground. The nibbled portion, if large enough, can be grown in a prepared hole as usual. A small portion can be potted into a large pot and then 'grown on' for another year (Figure 20).

Figure 20. Nibbling. A spade is pushed in deep on four sides of the piece of viticella to be removed. Using a spade a cube of earth, including the piece of viticella, is removed.

PLATE 86. *C. viticella* 'Ascotiensis' produces an eye-catching clear blue flower.

Seeds

The seed, or achene, of the viticella clematis consists of a base containing the seed and a short tail. The new plant will resemble the parent plant but may be poorer; a few may be better.

Select the seed from good plants. These are produced late in the season. Viable seeds are plump. Non-viable seeds are thin and must be discarded. The seed of the viticellas are best kept until the following spring. If they are stored they should be kept in a polythene bag, labelled and put into a refrigerator, where they can be chilled below 4°C (40°F) but not frozen.

In spring the seed will germinate in a seed medium in seed pans. Prick out as soon as the seedlings can be handled and put into a soil-based compost. Seeds of the viticella clematis will usually germinate quickly and produce seedlings in one season. Seedlings are potted up into small pots, 'potted on' to larger pots, and in one or two years will produce a bloom.

Chance seedings

When hoeing keep an eye out for the chance seedlings of viticellas. The seedlings may have come from a nearby plant or may have come from a cross between two of your clematis in the garden. Most of the seedlings will be worthless even though unique. To be worthwhile a new clematis must display characteristics not yet available. However, well-known viticellas, such as 'Margaret Hunt', have come from this happening. Seedlings are treated as in the section above.

Hybridising

Some amateur gardeners have the time denied the nurseries, and turn their hands to hybridising, which can be very successful. Here an entirely new plant is produced by crossing one plant with another. For those who have the knowledge and the time this is the most exciting aspect of clematis culture. It produces something unique and valuable. The principles are the same as for hybridising in any genus and an interested reader should consult the specialist literature.

Special Care of the Large-Flowered Viticella Clematis

The large-flowered viticellas are not as robust as plants of the far commoner small and medium-sized clematis. Occasionally they may develop stem rot (clematis wilt). This will never kill your plant if you follow the advice given here in two respects.

I The First Two Years

Care during this period, more than at any other time, guarantees the growth of a fine large viticella plant. The gardener should concentrate on producing a healthy plant rather than producing bloom.

In the first two years care must be exercised to water sufficiently. Each plant must receive at least 10 litres (2 gallons) of water per week. A rich fertiliser is not required in the first year as the plant is going to be given sufficient nutrient in the soil. However liquid fertiliser can be applied once a week during the growing period. During the second year more fertiliser can be given.

II Stem Rot (Clematis Wilt) Develops

A clematis can wilt for a number of reasons. If the stem is cut across by physical effort it will wilt above the cut. Deprived of water the stems will wilt. Vine weevil eating the roots of the clematis will kill the plant and cause the stems to wilt. Lastly the condition of stem rot will cause stems to wilt.

PLATE 87. A branch of red *C. viticella* 'Ernest Markham' glows against dark green holly.

Stem rot is caused by the actions of a fungus acting on a plant vulnerable to it. The vulnerability was introduced by *Clematis lanuginosa*, extensively used in hybridising programmes with clematis in the last century, and still in the breeding programmes today. In the case of the stem rot fungus the necessary conditions are something like this:

It needs the plump green stems of a clematis plant in its first two years, which is about to flower. With the green stems it likes a temperature of about 23°C, humidity and, if possible, a damaged part of the stem where it can get in. A clematis that has grown for two to three years is less likely to be attacked as the fungus cannot penetrate its now woody stems.

The fungus flourishes in a way that does maximum damage quickly: it works right across the stem killing as it goes and penetrates 2-5cm (1-2in). So it cuts off the sap and naturally the plant above the damage will wilt in days. Your leaves and flowers will hang limply and then turn brown as will the stem. The rotting is always at a node, usually low down near the ground. The affected node may on the outside have a little slime over it. Making a clean slice vertically up the stem reveals the damage. The final answer to clematis wilt is to hybridise with clematis that have no *C. lanuginosa* in their background. In the meantime what does the gardener do? Fortunately there is a lot that can be done:

PLATE 88. *C. viticella* 'Voluceau' is a neglected beauty.

a) If 'stem rot' strikes look down the stem to below any wilting leaves, a point which may be near ground level or even below. Cut the stem at this position, collect and burn it. The fungus is often present on the leaves of clematis.

b) It is important to emphasise that usually it is not 'stem rot' that kills a plant, but a gardener! This is because many assume a plant is dead and neglect it and so it dies. Instead, keep watering and in no time new stems appear. If you are unlucky a plant can wilt a couple of times more, but in the end you will have a strong plant.

c) Once your clematis has woody brown stems it is unusual for them to be attacked as they have strong defensive reactions against 'stem rot'. But branch stems can still be affected, and also their leaves. So if they are, cut them off and burn them.

d) You can stop a plant wilting altogether. Fungicides have been developed against 'stem rot'. In the case of the large flowered viticellas the incidence of stem rot is low and preventative measures not justified. But if you wish to employ preventative measures fungicides can be used containing the following active agents: carbendazim, thiophanate-methyl in 0.2% suspension, chlorothalonil, Fenpropimorph, propiconazole, Dichlorfluanide and Captafol. Unfortunately over-cautious governments keep removing fungicides from the commercial markets.

Some of the above have to be sprayed on the plants but it is better to use systemic fungicides and put these in the ground to avoid inhaling them. Give the plant a good watering first then sprinkle the fungicide from a watering can. Water the fungicide into the ground so as to reach the roots. Start in April. Do it every month until September. One last point: change your fungicide often as the fungus may develop immunity to a particular one.

Round the Year Care of Viticella Clematis

Mid-winter
Prepare clematis beds to be planted in early spring. Dig holes in preparation for planting later. Order tools, peat, manure, fertilisers, chemicals, etc.
Water any plants liable to dry out.
Establish, or bring up to date, a plan showing location of the viticella clematis.

Late Winter
Divide or nibble viticella clematis and replant (when conditions allow).
Water plants liable to dry out.
Check name labels on all viticellas.

Early Spring
Plant viticellas if conditions allow.
Prune the viticella clematis to the ground if there is no danger of frost damage to new shoots.
Weed beds.

Mid-spring
Apply general fertiliser to the clematis.
Start watering programme.

Late spring
Apply mulch of manure or other suitable material to the clematis.
Layer viticella stems kept unpruned for the purpose.
Continue watering programme.

Early summer
Apply second feeding of fertiliser.
Continue watering programme.

Mid-summer
Cut clematis for the house.
Continue watering programme.

Late summer
Cut flowers for the house.
Continue watering programme.

Early autumn
Gather clematis seed for spring sowing.
Prepare clematis beds if planting in autumn is desired.
Reduce watering when possible.

Mid-autumn
Tidy beds.
Plant clematis if autumn planting desired.
Reduce watering programme.
If viticella plants are unsightly on their supports, prune stems to 1m (3ft), tie together and place out of sight if possible.

Late autumn
Protect clematis in Cold Zone.

Early winter
Plan spring clematis planting and order plants.
Water plants liable to dry out.

A Reminder

In order to make the text useful in both hemispheres, plant flowering times, etc, are described in terms of seasons, not months. The following table translates seasons into months for the two hemispheres.

TABLE II

Northern Hemisphere		Southern Hemisphere
Mid-winter	January	Mid-summer
Late winter	February	Late summer
Early spring	March	Early autumn
Mid-spring	April	Mid-autumn
Late spring	May	Late autumn
Early summer	June	Early winter
Mid-summer	July	Mid-winter
Late summer	August	Late winter
Early autumn	September	Early spring
Mid-autumn	October	Mid-spring
Late autumn	November	Late spring
Early winter	December	Early summer

PLATE 89. *C. viticella* 'Madame Julia Correvon' and rose 'Pink Perpétue' are companions on a pergola.

PLATE 90. *C. viticella* 'Madame Julia Correvon' and rose 'New Dawn'.

CHAPTER SEVEN
Displaying Viticellas

There is no garden, however small, that cannot benefit from planting at least half a dozen viticella clematis. We can look at the garden as it is and ask questions such as where do I need interest, or colour, or tall plants, or fragrance? Could I use a viticella clematis? Or where are the gaps in my garden, and can they be filled by a viticella?

Principles of Display

Choosing the Right Neighbours

Adequate space must be allowed for the viticella and the plants around it; not the space required at planting but on a projection of three to four years. Viticellas and their neighbours should have approximately the same vigour or one will kill the other in time. If it is possible, it is best to plant the viticella close to plants of similar pruning habits. It makes life easier if the clematis and their neighbours require the same soil, fertilizers, water, light, and even fungicides. Height of clematis and

PLATE 91. The fragrance of *C. viticella* 'Triternata Rubromarginata' is overwhelming. It is seen on a wall at the Bagatelle Gardens, Paris.

neighbours can vary; if short, clematis can clothe the legs of a taller plant, or vice versa. Clematis rarely look well in formal rows.

A clematis must withstand the temperature you expect in the garden in winter. This is usually no problem with the viticellas which can flourish in the harshest climates down to -40°C in winter. Winter protection is discussed elsewhere (page 118).

Fragrant clematis should be planted near doors and paths, where the scent is likely to be picked up by the gardener and other passers-by. In the Viticella Group *C.* 'Triternata Rubromarginata' is outstanding for scent.

Some of us will feel that our gardens are full of interest and colour in the late spring and summer and it is best, therefore, to concentrate on the early and late-flowering clematis. Viticellas flower after mid-summer, when colour is diminishing, and bring a dramatic new show like the montana clematis in spring.

Colour
Colour theory is a complex subject and has been covered in some detail in the companion volume *The Rose and The Clematis as Good Companions.* The applications of colour theory to viticellas will be discussed here.

Yellow is not a colour available to this group; only the Orientalis Group has yellow flowers. But the viticellas have a good range of other colours from white to pink, red, to light blue and dark blue. The blue clematis complement the many yellow flowers to be found in roses and shrubs. Predominant colours are set out in the table overleaf.

TABLE III

WHITE PREDOMINANT	PINK PREDOMINANT	RED PREDOMINANT	LIGHT BLUE PREDOMINANT	DARK BLUE PREDOMINANT
'Alba Luxurians'	'Etoile Rose'	'Abundance'	'Emilia Plater'	'Viticella'
'Betty Corning'	'Margaret Hunt'	'Flore Pleno'	'Prince Charles'	'Blue Belle'
campaniflora	'Margot Koster'	'Jenny Caddick'	'Ascotiensis'	'Blue Boy'
'Elvan'	'Mrs T. Lundell'	'Kermesina'	'Perle d'Azur'	'Etoile Violette'
'Huldine'	'Tango'	'Kosmiczeskaja	'Blekitny Aniol'	'Hendersonii'
'Little Nell'	'Triternata Rubro-	Melodija'		'Polish Spirit'
'Minuet'	marginata'	'Madame Julia		'Venosa Violacea'
'Pagoda'	'Mrs Spencer Castle'	Correvon'		'Lady Betty Balfour'
		'Purpura Plena		
		Elegans'		
		'Royal Velours'		
		'Södertälje'		
		'Ville de Lyon'		
		'Ernest Markham'		
		'Madame Grangé'		
		'Voluceau'		

In looking at the colour of the flower account must be taken of the colours of both the tepals and the stamens. Dark stamens against red in 'Kermesina' give a quite different effect to the light stamens against red in 'Madame Julia Correvon'.

PLATE 92. *C. viticella* 'Madame Julia Correvon' has a light centre.

PLATE 93. *C. viticella* 'Kermesina' has a dark centre.

The dark stamens in red 'Kermesina' lead to a quite different effect from that given by the light stamens of red 'Madame Julia Correvon'. The colour of the viticella must be matched to its background. This can be the colour of another flower which you may wish to contrast or complement. It may be the green of another plant – this is very common in the garden and an easy combination. Or is it a wall? A white viticella will be lost on a white wall, blue or pink looks well in that situation. Pink or red do not blend well with a brick wall.

Is the plant to flower in shade, or more acceptably, semi-shade? White, pink or light blue will lighten up semi-shade. Is the plant to flower in full sun? The light colours, white, pink, light blue, will tend to fade quickly, so use the strong reds and dark blues.

The light blue and dark blue viticellas benefit enormously from being lit up by contrasting orange and yellow. But use the yellow sparingly, in the ratio of approximately one part yellow to four parts blue.

PLATE 94. The fine single rose 'Mermaid' contrasts in the right proportions with *C. viticella* 'Perle d'Azur'.

PLATE 95. Viticellas 'Venosa Violacea', 'Prince Charles' and 'Madame Julia Correvon' mingle to great effect.

Too much red can be overwhelming in a garden. Tone it down with plenty of green leafy background.

Contrasts of colour tend to produce restlessness; complementary colours are restful. Some contrasting colours are white and red, yellow and mauve, orange and blue, red and green. Some complementary colours are pink and light blue, red and mauve, pink and red, cream and lilac, white and lilac, pink and deep pink.

For real drama plant a number of plants of the same colour together, for example three to four plants of 'Perle d'Azur' on a wall, or three to four plants of 'Margot Koster' over a bank of heathers.

If viticellas are planted close together the colours can be kept apart, but allowing them to mingle can be very pleasing.

It is also possible to arrange a sequence of colours by placing an early-flowering viticella such as 'Madame Julia Correvon', followed by 'Little Nell' which can then be followed by late-flowering 'Lady Betty Balfour'

The Flowering Periods
The five ways of growing viticellas with support plants are:
1. **before** the support plant flowers
2. **when** the support plant flowers
3. **after** the support plant flowers
4. **under** the support plant
5. **near** the support plant

PLATE 96. Viticellas can be planted with clematis of a different group. Here 'John Huxtable' of the Jackmanii Group contrasts attractively with *C. viticella* 'Perle d'Azur'.

1. The flowering of the viticellas can be related to the background planting. If the background plant is yet to flower, the viticella can give colour to a background tree, shrub, rose, creeping plants or climbers. This is the first way of using the viticellas – **before** the host plant flowers.
2. If the viticella is to flower at the same time as its background plant an attempt must be made to match the colours of each. This is the second way of using the viticellas on host plants – **when** the host plant flowers.
3. The viticellas may flower after a host plant flowers, for example large rhododendrons, dull and colourless, cry out for the colour of the viticellas. This is the third way of using the viticellas with host plants – **after** the host plant flowers.
4. Some host plants, for example a climbing rose, can be very tall. A short viticella can grow under such a plant and clothe its bottom few feet – 'Hendersonii' or 'Blue Boy'. This is the fourth way of growing viticellas – **below** the host plant.
5. A viticella can also grow beside other plants and contribute to the general colour scheme: viticellas on supports can enliven a shrubbery or rose shrubs, or a border. This is the fifth way of using viticellas with other plants – **near** those plants.

The flowering period of the viticellas can be extended by using other clematis with them; a chapter has been devoted to this. Further extension can take place by the two pruning techniques already discussed.

Late flowering hybrid 'John Huxtable' blends well with 'Perle d' Azur' .

PLATE 97. Viticellas 'Alba Luxurians' and 'Ernest Markham' cover a pillar in the garden of Mike Brown, near Oxford, UK.

Using Viticellas on Host Plants

Some viticellas are large plants but sometimes the host plant is larger and more than one viticella can then be used. If one is used it should be planted 1m (3ft) away from the host plant and led to it by canes. You can plant one viticella at 62cm (2ft) on either side of the host. Another, at the same time, or later, can be planted opposite the host and 1m (3ft) away. So three clematis are possible for each host plant (Figure 21).

In multiple planting the viticellas can be selected so that all flower together or in sequence over a period of time. If they flower together there is a maximum impact for a short period. To obtain a sequence use three viticellas, choosing early, middle and late-flowering varieties. Another sequence can be obtained by using early or late-flowering clematis from other clematis groups.

You can either plant different varieties of viticellas or all the same. They can be of similar or different colours such as a group of three different red viticellas or a grouping of pink, white, and violet ones.

In multiple planting the viticellas can be kept apart so that a particular type and colour is seen from a particular direction. Even more effective is to allow the three viticellas to mingle and thus

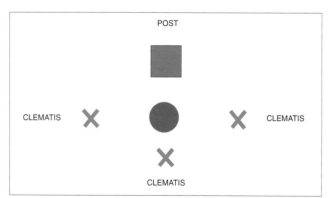

Figure 21. Two or three clematis (X) can be positioned near a host plant (●).

PLATE 98. 'Minuet' makes an exciting picture against a white wall in the garden of Beth Chatto, near Colchester, UK.

produce, with the host, a great centre of interest.

It is often said that a clematis should be planted on the shaded side of the object it is meant to cover. The theory is that the sun will draw the plant in the right direction. Unfortunately you may find that there is so much shade that the viticella makes poor growth. In these circumstances it is best to grow the viticellas at the side of the shrub and guide it where you want it to go.

The number of clematis for each host – which can range from two to six or more – depends on the size of the host and the vigour of the clematis.

The viticellas planted between host plants will often need the support of a pillar, a pyramid, an umbrella, a waterfall or cascade frame (Figure 22). These will be discussed shortly.

The viticella used in the arrangements mentioned can be pruned in two stages in the Standard Zone. In Stage 1, the autumn growth is cut out at a height of 91cm (3ft). Gentle tugging will ensure that the growth on the host will come away and can be

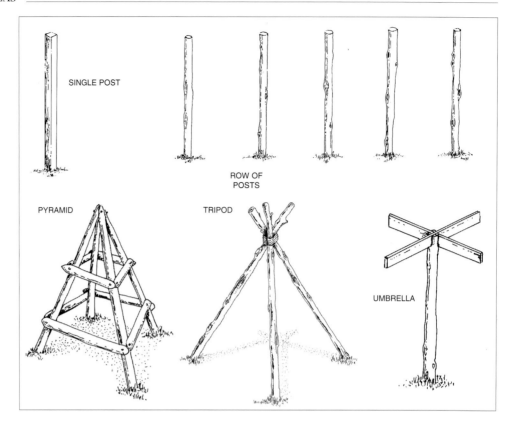

Figure 22. Using posts.

Figure 23. A metal spike

Figure 24. Bolt down fixing for a post

burnt. The remaining stems are brought together with a tie and hidden at the edge of the support plant. In Stage 2, in the spring, the clematis is finally pruned to the ground. So look carefully at your garden landscape, and in particular the micro-climate (the immediate environment of a plant), and consider where you can enhance your garden by the judicious planting of these rewarding, beautiful plants. Carefully chosen, there is a viticella for every aspect of the house, whichever way it faces.

Physical Supports for Viticellas

Wood
A simple way of giving support is by the use of posts or poles which can be used at points in the garden where there is no natural support. Poles can give height to a display of viticellas in a herbaceous border. Again the post with clematis can be a special feature on a lawn.

Posts should be of hard wood. They must be buried deep enough into the ground so that they can withstand not only the weight of the clematis but also the stress of the wind. It is possible to use a metal spike, which is sunk into the ground or concrete or a metal plate; the post fitting into this has a longer life, is easier to replace, and does not move when under stress (Figures 23, 24).

The viticella needs to be tied to the pole and to make this possible the pole should be surrounded by wire netting or wire running vertically.

Much ingenuity can be employed over the use of posts. A single post or a row of posts can be placed along the length of a border, along the side of a path, at intervals in a shrubbery, or as a partition between one part of the garden and another. Three posts can be brought together to form a pyramid or tripod on which the clematis climbs (Figure 22).

Another interesting way of employing posts is to have an umbrella at the top (such

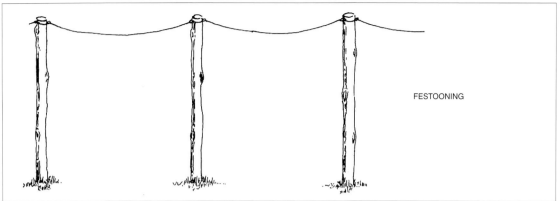

Figure 25.
Festooning.

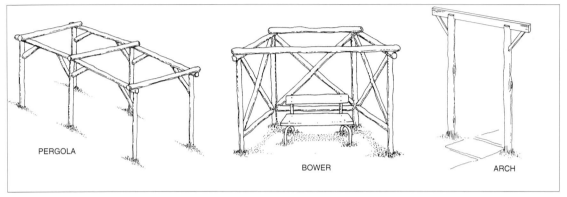

Figure 26.
Wood
structures.

as an inverted hanging basket). Yet another attractive way of display is to run a rope or a chain or wire between two posts; the viticella is encouraged to run along the support between the two posts thus giving the effect of festooning (Figure 25).

Two posts together with a third pole above make an arch. The arch should be 2-2.5m (7-8ft) tall to allow comfortable access. Arches can make an arbour, or bower, or gazebo, or rotunda. Posts can also be used to make a pergola. It can be of simple rustic posts or hardwood (Figure 26).

The same principles apply to clematis on wooden fences, trellises or screens. There are many types of fences – close boarded, paling, post and rail, post and wire, chain link, interwoven panels. A trellis should be supported on walls by battens.

Metal
Metal supports can match all the uses of the wood supports. Single metal structures take the place of a pole or pillar. Combinations of single structures make arches, arbours, pergolas, bowers, gazebos and fences, including chain link fences (Figure 27).

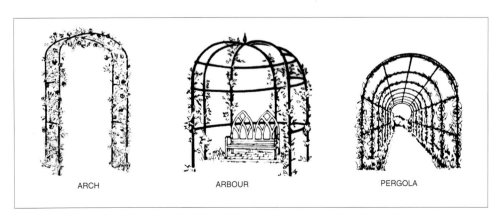

Figure 27. Metal
structures.

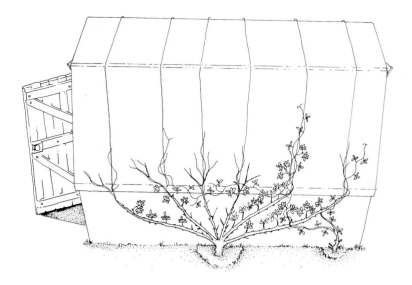

Figure 28. A viticella can
beautify a shed.

Stone and Brick

Stone structures can match most of the uses of the wooden structures. We can use stone and bricks to make pillars, arches, porches, bowers, pergolas, gazebos, colonnades and, of course, walls.

Walls

Walls can be those of a house, a garage or an outbuilding. They can surround a garden or divide it. Clematis look particularly effective on short walls running alongside steps or climbing over balustrades.

A clematis can be alone on a wall but this is not ideal as in winter all that can be seen is almost barren stalks. It is more effective, though, to allow clematis to climb up existing climbing plants on the walls. A third way is to plant the clematis between climbing plants.

When planting on a wall, a number of points must be borne in mind. The clematis, as was discussed earlier, must be planted well away from the wall – at least 60cm (2ft) – and led back by string, wire or cane. The perspective is enhanced if the spread of the clematis is roughly equivalent to its height. Should the clematis prove too high for the wall, the upper tresses can be led down again towards the ground by wire, string or cane, giving a waterfall effect. Low-growing clematis can be planted to hide any bare legs of a viticella.

Roofs

The roof of a shed is one of the most difficult areas to beautify. Wire it in horizontal lengths and the clematis are encouraged to grow along them, tied in, giving sensational results (Figure 28).

Additional Supports

Useful structures in shrubberies are posts, pyramids, and umbrellas near the shrubs. Some use strong netting hung between two posts up which clematis can climb. It is possible to stretch netting horizontally between supports allowing the clematis to climb upwards on the netting (Figure 29).

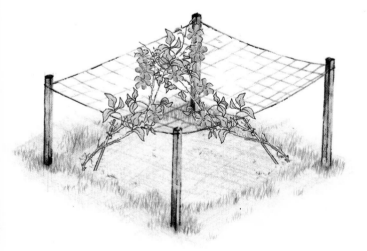

Figure 29. Viticellas can climb through and on netting stretched between posts.

PLATE 99. *C. viticella* 'Prince Charles' shares a wall with rose 'Parkdirektor Riggers'.

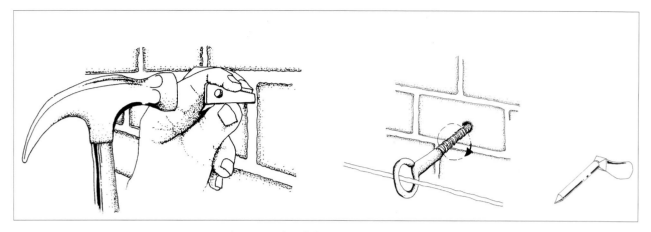

Figure 30. Masonry nail wall fixings. Drive in vine eye at junction of the bricks. A screw eye supports wire.

Training Clematis

It is necessary to have strong horizontal wire supports to hold clematis on walls. The simplest support is a wire running between two nails. It is much better to use galvanised nails, or better still, masonry nails (Figure 30) on which there is a clip that the wire can run through. A stronger support comes from using vine eyes driven into the walls at intervals and through which the wire can run (Figure 30). But the strongest support is given by screw eyes. A hole is drilled in the wall where a rawlplug is inserted and into which a screw is turned (Figure 30). The wire should be of a gauge strong enough to withstand the weight of the clematis, and the force of the wind. It should be secured at 1.2m (4ft) intervals and be 45cm (1½ft) apart. The wire should be at least 5cm (2in) away from the wall as this allows the stem of the viticella to reach behind the wire and cling to it. When it is necessary to repair or decorate the wall the clematis will fall away easily in one piece and lie tidily on the ground.

Tying in Clematis

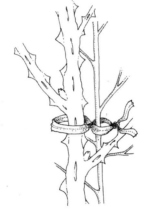

Figure 31. The tie goes round the support and is gently twisted once to close the loop. The viticella is now placed between the open ends of the tie and these ends are gently twisted once or twice as necessary.

The clematis is tied directly to the support or to a host plant already on the support. A number of ties can be used. Raffia can be used where the tie does not need to be permanent, though green string is preferable and unobtrusive. Paper-covered ties can be used with clematis that are going to be hard pruned in the autumn. They are impermanent and can only be used for a year. Plastic coated wire is permanent and quick to use. It should not be allowed to squeeze the stem too tightly and room must be allowed for growth in the diameter of the stem. The gardener soon becomes adept at using these plastic ties (Figure 31).

Natural Support for Viticellas

Viticellas look best climbing into or over other large plants. A great range of natural supports is available. They can also be useful adorning a patio or in containers. Each aspect will be taken in turn.

Trees

Viticellas are large plants but not so large that they can climb into a large tree as easily as a montana clematis. They fit admirably into small trees (Plate 100).

Some general principles need to be borne in mind in growing clematis into trees.

PLATE 100. *C. viticella* 'Abundance' climbs a conifer tree in the gardens of Burford House, Tetbury, UK.

The tree should be well established before the viticella grows into it; the weight of a viticella in a strong wind is considerable which the tree must be robust enough to bear. The viticella should never be so vigorous as to suffocate the tree, or vice versa; the two must be matched. The clematis should be allowed to grow as naturally as possible in the tree; however, quite often, judicious tying in of the clematis can help the final shape. Smaller trees do best with viticella clematis that require pruning in the autumn. This allows the tree to be tidied up for the winter

Figure 32. With a vertical growing tree you can plant within 1m (3ft) of the trunk.

and also reduces the weight on them during winter storms.

The aim is to bring interest and colour to a tree which is not blooming and would otherwise be dull and uninteresting. Not only must account be taken of the colour of the clematis but also of the colour and form of the clematis foliage. In general, pale-coloured or fluorescent clematis do best against dark trees and the brighter-coloured plants against the lighter ones.

Evergreen Trees

An evergreen tree particularly benefits from a combination with a clematis as, of course, it rarely develops spectacular flowers. A dark columnar conifer looks magnificent clothed in white, pink and light red viticellas (Plate 100). Try 'Etoile Violette', light blue viticellas and 'Royal Velours' with yellow conifers. These trees frequently need to be wired to support the branches against heavy snow in the winter. The clematis can thus be tied in to the wire and guided to twine round and round the conifer foliage. With smaller holly trees try 'Huldine'; its white bloom will show up against the dark foliage. For a variegated holly, pink and red viticella varieties would be suitable.

PLATE 101. *C. viticella* 'Prince Charles' climbs into *Pyrus salicifolia* 'Pendula'.

Figure 33. With a globe-shaped tree planting must be at the periphery, out of the shade. Clematis has support from a cane.

Deciduous Trees

Of all the deciduous trees, none can beat *Pyrus salicifolia* 'Pendula' as a support for clematis. Its silvery leaves are a natural foil and almost every coloured viticella will appeal against this background, except perhaps white ones (Plate 101). *Prunus subhirtella* 'Autumnalis' is a great joy with its white or pink blossom through the winter, but for the rest of the year its leaves are somewhat insipid. The viticellas can climb into it and transform it; the clematis can be pruned back for winter. Most of the prunus tend to flower briefly in the spring and can have similar treatment. This would apply also to the *Crataegus* (hawthorns) and *Malus* (ornamental crabs). The false acacia *Robinia pseudoacacia* 'Frisia' (Plate 102) needs a foil for its glowing yellow foliage and here we can consider the light blue viticellas and the dark blues. The flowers of *Laburnum* are early and thus its foliage would benefit from a clematis later; 'Ville de Lyon' is suitable. The *Sorbus* (Rowan) group tends to have fern-like foliage and a *Clematis* can greatly enhance it; 'Purpurea Plena Elegans' is a suitable choice. The *Acer* (maples), with leaves of light hues, will benefit from viticella cultivars selected to match the leaves. The opportunities are infinite.

Planting Near a Tree

It must be remembered that the soil and conditions around a tree are not very kind to a clematis; the soil is often dry and has been exhausted by the tree and may also be shaded. All these deficiencies have to be countered.

It is usual to advise that clematis should be planted on the shady side of the tree so that the light at the other side of the tree will pull the clematis through it. Furthermore, it is assumed that the clematis will benefit from any moisture in the shade. Unhappily the shade is often of such depth that the clematis refuses to take off. So it is often better to plant on the sunny side of the tree and lead the clematis into the tree by canes or string; and once it has reached the tree, it will then take its own course.

A heavy mulching is necessary to compensate for the sun drying the ground. How close the viticella is planted depends on the shape of the tree. An upright tree, like *Robinia pseudoacacia* 'Frisia' for instance, has roots that go straight into the ground and the branches offer little shade close to the tree. In this case the viticella can be planted within 1m (3ft) of the tree trunk (Figure 32). A globe-shaped tree such as *Pyrus salicifolia* 'Pendula' has deep shade around its trunk. Here the viticellas must be planted at the edge of the tree out of the shade. This may be 2-2½m (6-8ft) from

PLATE 102. *C. viticella* 'Emilia Plater' climbs into a dark shrub.

the trunk, and led into the branches above it (Figure 33). In this way the viticellas will have sun and good soil for initial growth and the rain will reach them.

Even when the clematis stems are woody and strong, a cane should always be kept alongside the stem. Then it is less easy for someone to blunder against the stem and break it; games on the lawn can bring damage.

The size of a tree will determine the number of viticellas that can climb into it. Consider multiple planting for dramatic effect: two or three of the same viticellas can be used, or two or three different varieties flowering in sequence will give colour over a longer period.

PLATE 103. Viticellas 'Abundance' (red) and 'Etoile Violette' (blue) climb into the yellow leaves of *Robinia pseudoacacia* 'Frisia'.

Shrubs

The general principles are as for trees. The shrub should be allowed to reach its optimum size and height before clematis is carried into it when it must also be able to withstand the weight of the clematis. A too vigorous clematis can kill a shrub while too weak a one can be killed by its host plant. The shrub and the clematis must also be matched for flower and foliage. Viticellas can be pruned in the autumn and are ideal if the shrubs need to be free of clematis during the winter. Shrubs of dark foliage will match best with light coloured viticellas such as the pinks, the whites and the light blues (Plate 102). Shrubs with light foliage on the other hand are more suitable for a strongly coloured viticella (Plate 103). A shrub may be able to carry more than one viticella.

A long hedge can be spectacular with viticellas peeping over it. Plant them 1m (3ft) away from the hedge and lead them to the hedge with canes. Once the viticellas have clung to the hedge the canes can be taken away. Viticellas can also be pruned in such a way as to make growth a short distance from the ground. This gives the viticella extra height and so helps it on to the hedge. This was discussed earlier under 'Pruning' (pages 125-126). Viticellas are supreme for this purpose as they can be trimmed back in the autumn, thus leaving the hedge unencumbered and ready for trimming. The trimming can be repeated in the spring before the viticellas reach it.

Many shrubs, either before, at, or after flowering, can be used as hosts for viticellas. A few suggestions are *Cytisus* (broom), *Berberis* (barberry), *Cornus* (dogwood), *Cotinus* (smoke tree), *Cotoneaster*, *Elaeagnus*, *Escallonia*, *Magnolia*, *Viburnum* and all the shrub roses. We need an international campaign to clothe dreary rhododendrons with viticellas after mid-summer!

Planting Near a Shrub

The clematis must be planted at least 60cm (2ft) away from the edge of the shrub and led to it on a cane, string or wire. Wire can be pegged near the clematis and the wire or green string carried over the shrub to the other side in the direction in which you want the viticella to grow. Several supports can be used if necessary to criss-cross the support plant (Figure 34). It should be planted on the sunny side to

PLATE 104. *C. viticella* 'Venosa Violacea' clambers over low growing *Senecio* in a border.

encourage growth, and given a good mulching to retain moisture in the sun. The point of exit of the clematis from the soil must be marked with a cane, otherwise it is likely to be hoed up when you work on the shrubbery. Careful attention must be given to watering.

Some climbing shrubs make excellent companions and support for the viticellas. Overall, some suitable companions are *Buddleia alternifolia*, the foliage of *Camellia*

Figure 34. The viticella is planted 1m (2-3ft) away from the shrub or shrub rose and guided over it with green wire or green twine.

Figure 35. A viticella can be grown on a support in a shrubbery.

japonica, the trumpet vine *Campsis radicans* (with strong blue viticellas such as 'Blue Belle' and 'Polish Spirit'), *Ceanothus* after flowering (they flower too early to match the viticella flowers), the foliage of the *Chaenomeles*, *Cotoneaster horizontalis*, foliage of *Garrya elliptica*, *Hedera* (ivies), *Hydrangea petiolaris* (during and after flowering), the *Jasminum* (jasmines), or the climbing *Lonicera* (honeysuckles), the foliage of wall *Magnolia*, wall *Pyracantha*, *Solanum* and above all, *Wisteria* (the deep blue viticellas are magnificent in the foliage of the *Wisteria*). The viticellas can be pruned down in the autumn cleaning up the host plants.

Borders

Viticellas can first be used to give height to a border by growing them on a support such as a post, a tripod, or an umbrella (Figure 35). The less vigorous, but continuous flowering viticellas are ideal for this and include 'Pagoda', 'Betty Corning', 'Etoile Rose', 'Hendersonii', and 'Blue Boy'. The same treatment to 'Triternata Rubromarginata' produces a mound of fragrance that defies description.

PLATE 105. Climbing rose 'Golden Showers' combines well with all the blue viticellas.

159

PLATE 106. Rugosa (shrub) rose 'Scabrosa' is reliable for almost continuous blooming.

The second use is to allow the viticellas to clamber amongst the plants and roses, even near ground level (Plate 109). Some guidance can be given the clematis by tying it to a series of short canes which have been put on the line you wish the clematis to take (Figure 36). Again, the viticellas are pruned away in the autumn cleaning up the host plants.

Figure 36. Clematis can be guided the way you want them to go between plants by tying their stems to green canes placed in a line.

Creeping or Ground Cover Plants

Heathers, dwarf conifers, potentillas, ivies, senecios (Plate 104), ground-cover roses make excellent partners to the viticellas, and these make colour when the hosts are out of flower. Guide the viticella over the hosts with canes in the way described for border plants. Use the viticellas with an open rather than a bell-shaped flower and avoid the very vigorous ones such as 'Blue Belle' and 'Polish Spirit'. More than one

PLATE 107. Floribunda (cluster) rose 'Mountbatten' has a long flowering period.

PLATE 108. *C. viticella* 'Etoile Violette' climbs strongly into a pergola.

viticella can be used depending on the size of bed. A dramatic effect of a sea of colour is produced by using a number of the same variety such as 'Perle d'Azur'. Prune the viticellas away in the autumn to tidy the bed.

In the nineteenth century it was usual for gardeners to use beds for creeping clematis alone. They were allowed to clamber over brushwood laid for this purpose. For the rest of the year potted plants were moved in to give colour to the space

Roses

These are the ideal companions for clematis and for viticellas. So important is the partnership that a companion volume *The Rose and the Clematis as Good Companions* has been devoted to it. The principles and procedures of growing are exactly as for trees and shrubs.

Climbing, shrub, bedding and ground cover roses all make companions in the following forms. A number of readily available, easily grown, well-tried roses in each category will be listed for the use of the reader.

PLATE 109. *C. viticella* 'Royal Velours' meanders through creeping rose 'Nozomi'.

TABLE IV

Climbing Roses

WHITE/CREAM	ORANGE/YELLOW	PINK	RED	BI-COLOUR
'Albéric Barbier'	'Casino'	'Compassion'	'Dublin Bay'	'Handel'
'Iceberg'	'Emily Gray'	'Galway Bay'	'Guinée'	
'Mme Alfred Carrière'	'Golden Showers'	'Pink Perpétue'	'Parkdirektor	
'New Dawn'	'Mermaid'	'Summer Wine'	Riggers'	
	'Schoolgirl'			

SELECTION. If only room for one – 'Compassion'.
If only room for three – 'Compassion', 'New Dawn', 'Pink Perpétue'.
If only room for six – 'Compassion', 'New Dawn', 'Pink Perpétue',
'Handel', 'Golden Showers', 'Mermaid'.

Early Climbing Roses
A number of climbing roses flower very early. They cannot be used to match the colour of the flowers of the viticellas but they make ideal support for them when they flower and the viticellas put colour on the flowerless roses.

YELLOW	PINK
'Gloire de Dijon' 'Maigold'	'Albertine' 'Meg' 'Madame Grégoire Staechelin'

Shrub Roses

The shrub roses fall into three groups for planning:

1. The **very early** flowering shrubs, for example 'Canary Bird' and 'Frühlingsgold', bloom early and after flowering are available as support for viticellas. They flower too early to be available to match the flowering of the viticella clematis.
2. The **mid-season** shrub roses that flower once. Some flower late enough to be matched with those of the viticellas. All are available for support after flowering.
3. The **repeat-flowering** shrubs. Viticellas can be matched with these roses for colour at flowering and all the shrub roses are available for support to the viticellas.

Use the viticellas in the way described earlier for shrubs.

Twenty shrub roses are named here. Three flower very early – 'Canary Bird', 'Nevada' and 'Frühlingsgold'. Two can continue to flower very late – 'Buff Beauty' and 'Felicia'. The remainder start flowering in mid-summer: of these some of the old roses will not repeat but the modern shrub roses will tend to do so. The shrubs vary in size from low, for example, 'Chinatown', to medium size 'Canary Bird', to large 'Frühlingsgold'. The shrub roses are listed here alphabetically and by colour groups.

TABLE V

Shrub Roses

WHITE	PINK	RED	YELLOW/ORANGE	PURPLE
'Madame Hardy' 'Moonlight' 'Nevada' 'Sally Holmes'	'Ballerina' 'Celesta' 'Fantin-Latour' 'Felicia' 'Königin von Dänemark'	'Fred Loads'	'Buff Beauty 'Canary Bird' 'Chinatown' 'Frühlingsgold' 'Graham Thomas'	'Roseraie de l'Hay'

SELECTION. One shrub rose to be grown – 'Canary Bird'.

Three shrub roses to be grown – 'Canary Bird', 'Frühlingsgold', 'Nevada'.

Bedding Roses

Use the viticellas as described earlier for borders.

Hundreds of roses are available. To make a selection of the best we must turn to the tables published under the authority of the Royal National Rose Society. The top six Hybrid Teas (HT) are taken with the top six Floribundas (cluster-flowerers) (FL) from their recommendations. In the latter group I have added a particular proven favourite – 'Pink Parfait'. The roses are listed in alphabetical order:

TABLE VI

Bedding Roses

NAME	COLOUR	NAME	COLOUR
'Elina' HT	Ivory with lemon centre	'Peace' HT	Yellow
'Fragrant Cloud' HT	Geranium red	'Pink Parfait' FL	Pink and cream
'Iceberg' FL	Pure white	'Savoy Hotel' HT	Light pink
'Just Joey' HT	Coppery orange	'Sexy Rexy' FL	Rose pink
'Korresia' FL	Yellow	'Silver Jubilee' HT	Salmon pink
'Margaret Merril' FL	Pearly white	'Trumpeter' FL	Bright red

SELECTION. If only one plant – 'Pink Parfait'
If only three plants – 'Pink Parfait', 'Peace', 'Just Joey'

PLATE 110. A selection of viticellas give vivid colouring in a floral decoration.

PLATE 111. *C. viticella* 'Madame Julia Correvon' combines harmoniously with climbing rose 'Compassion'.

Groundcover Roses

These short roses have been developed to fulfil a need to be trouble free, spreading, weed suppressing, and long flowering. All the viticellas can be trained through them as discussed for creeping plants. Good plants are:

NAME	COLOUR
'Essex	Reddish-pink with white centre
'Flower Carpet'	Deep pink and white
'Grouse'	Blush-white
'Kent'	White
'Nozomi'	Blush-pink and white
'Suma'	Red and pink
'White Flower Carpet'	White

SELECTION: If one plant to be grown – 'Flower Carpet'
If three plants to be grown – 'Flower Carpet' , 'Grouse' , 'Nozomi'

Figure 37. A container can be wrapped in a layer of bubble polythene and an outer layer of hessian or netting for winter protection.

Patio and Containers

If there is a choice between making a hole in the patio for a viticella or planting in a container, choose the hole. All clematis will flourish in the ground beneath the patio; the stonework makes an ideal mulch. Water the hole, go away happily for the weekend. Return. Water again. Go away for a week. Furthermore the viticella will grow strongly in Mother Earth. The face of the hole can be beautified with stones, etc, but leave a small channel for the water to percolate from the rain falling on the patio.

Sometimes there is no choice. Containers have to be used. They can produce fine plants but only at the cost of laborious planting, continuous feeding and a regular, frequent, watering programme.

For the patio hole all the viticellas can be used, either alone or in companionship with climbing roses and shrubs.

The stronger-growing viticellas will quickly exhaust the soil in the container so the less vigorous viticellas must be used. The long-flowering bell-flowered 'Betty Corning' and 'Pagoda', the continuous flowering 'Blue Boy' and 'Hendersonii' are suitable as are light blue 'Prince Charles' and 'Blekitny Aniol'.

In the northern part of the Standard Zone and in the Cold Zone, containers will need protection in the winter, even to being taken indoors (Figure 37). In the Cold Zone some have adopted the practice of growing clematis, especially the Large Flowered, in containers so that they can be taken indoors in winter.

Cut Flowers

Most of the viticellas produce flowers with long stems making them suitable for cutting for flower arrangements. Some make striking cut flowers, 'Venosa Violacea' for instance. The bell-flowered viticellas have a delicate beauty. Viticellas can be arranged alone, in multi-coloured groups or with the flowers of other plants. They are very effective with roses. The many blue viticellas make a perfect foil for the yellow flowers of other plants.

PLATE 112. A posy of viticellas.

PLATE 113. Lost viticellas 'Rubra Grandiflora' (red) and 'Mrs James Bateman' (blue).

CHAPTER EIGHT
Some Lost Viticellas

From time to time new viticellas have been added to the group by crossing together, accidentally, or deliberately, or with other species.

Clematis viticella is a southern European native plant and interest in it has remained largely European. After 1860 with the rising interest in clematis, new viticellas were introduced throughout Europe and particularly in France and the United Kingdom. When clematis stem rot (wilt) became widespread in Europe

PLATE 114. Lost *viticella* 'Marmorata'. PLATE 115. Lost *viticella* 'Lady Bovill'.

from 1870 onwards it was natural to turn to the wilt-free viticellas. At the turn of the nineteenth century many new viticellas were produced, especially in France. In Britain just before World War II there was a spate of new viticellas from Gravetye Manor under Ernest Markham. As mentioned before, it is likely that many of Markham's introductions came from Morel in France. Since the Second World War some new viticellas have been introduced throughout Europe and hopefully this tendency will accelerate in an attempt to fill gardens with wilt-free clematis.

Unhappily, along the way, viticellas were lost due to a variety of reasons. The chief problem was a loss of interest in clematis at the end of the nineteenth century and into the twentieth century. As a result many clematis, including the newly developed viticellas, went out of production. Even Ernest Markham's introductions of the late 1930s were lost on his death during World War II.

Below are listed about 100 viticellas thought to be lost; their finding and reintroduction will give pleasure to all. Despite diligent searching in the American, Belgian, British, Dutch, French, and German literature, I do not claim that this is a final list; others may be able to add to it.

Included in the list is a digest of information, when known, culled from books and the horticultural press. Sometimes there is virtually no information while at other times there is a surprisingly large amount. The numbered references will give a start to a scholar wishing to follow up a particular clematis; they appear at the end of this chapter. The lost clematis are listed alphabetically.

List of Lost Viticellas

'ABENDSTERN'
Wine red. Medium size.[28a]
From Goos and Koehemann of Wiesbaden, Germany.*
*Schreck, R.M. (1996) Personal Communication.

'ALBA'
Carrière, E.A.. *Clematis viticella alba*.[25e & f]
Viticella Alba. New. Blooms 6-7cm across. White.[16b]
White. Four tepals. Carrière.[24]
The white Virgin's Bower (*Clematis viticella alba*). The various forms of the hardy, easily-grown Virgin's Bower deserve to be widely known and freely planted. They need no careful culture, but like a hedge, bush, fence, or something similar to climb over and hang their long festoons of blossom upon. The white form is now in flower, and proves a welcome companion to the crimson kind recently noted. Its flowers show a considerable advance in size upon those of the type, and although not of a true pure white colour, they are nearly so, there being just a faint suffusion of mauve in them.[10f]
A white variety of known species, to which it should prove a companion.[10g]
White flower 6-7cm across.[6]
Alba with white flowers.[28a]
White. Also called 'Viticella Alba', but not to be confused with the natural variety.[5]

'ALBA NOVA'
White.[28a]

'ALGER'
Four tepals. blue[24]

'AMETHYSTINA'
Jackman: A variety obtained from the crossing of *C. lanuginosa* and *C. viticella*, partaking more of the character of the latter parent, and having pale violet-blue flowers. It has not been sent out, and is now discarded.[13]
The blue flowers have curled petals, and are of a pale violet-blue colour; very beautiful.[12]
   One of the same batch of seedlings as *C. lanuginosa pallida*, but taking on more of the character of *Viticella*, the petals being erect instead of spreading, narrower, and more or less recurved at the margin. The flowers had, nevertheless, a bold and firm appearance, and were of a pale violet-blue colour. Commendation.[23m]
(Jackman), pale violet-blue. Discarded before 1877.[28a]

'ARABELLA'
Medium size. White.[28a]
(Lemoine). Double. White.[6]

'ARAGO'
(Lemoine). Violet purple.[28a]

'ARTS P. DU BUY'[27]
Red-violet. Middle darker.

'ASCANIO'
(Lemoine). Double, white with lilac edges.[6, 28a]

'ATRAGENOIDES'
Blue, paler towards centre.[28a]

'ATRORUBENS'
C. viticella 'Atrorubens' Hort. – A free-growing and free-blooming plant, moderately slender in growth. The leaves are pinnatisect, the flowers abundant and successional, about two inches across, semi-expanded, of a pleasing tint of rosy-crimson, with a tuft of pale green stamens, which form a very pretty contrast; it is, however, now superseded by *C. viticella rubra* grandiflora.[23m]
Rosy crimson.[2]
(This clematis was one of the parents of the famous *C.* 'Jackmannii'.)

'ATROVIOLACEA'
Carrière. Desirable hardy plant, but unfortunately named, as not species properly so called.[11]
Clematis atroviolacea - Carrière.[25f]
Deep violet.[28a]

'BOSKOOP'[10h]
Hort. (syn. *C. Boskoop seedling*, Hort.) (= *C.viticella* x *C.integrifolia*). A new race in 1892; growing 3-5ft; fls. blue, lavender, rose, reddish-rose.[2]

'C.H. JOOSTEN'
Blue.

'COERULEA'
Blue.[5]
C. integrifolia x *C. viticella*. Van Keef. Boskoop. 1897.[18]

'COERULEA GRANDIFLORA'
Azure-blue.[28b]

'COERULEA LUXURIANS'[18]

'CONTORTA'
Desirable hardy plant, but unfortunately named, as not species properly so called.[11]
Clematis contorta.[25f]
Pale lilac to mauve.[28a]

'COQUETTE'
(Lemoine). White.[28a]

'Coquette'.[22]
White. Of greater garden interest for their enhanced floral beauty are the hybrids of which *C. viticella* has been a parent. They include large-flowering forms such as 'Coquette'.[30]

'Cratère'
Cratère (Lemoine). Purple.[18]

'Crippsii'
C. crippsii, Cripps – A vigorous-growing plant, of free-flowering habit, belonging to the Viticella group, and having simple or ternate leaves, with broad cordate ovate leaflets. The flowers are of a deep bluish-mauve colour, very much resembling those of *C. tunbridgensis*, and altogether not equal in merit to that variety.[23a]

'C. van Kleef'[27]
Purple with pink.

'Darkie'
From Mr Ernest Markham, East Grinstead.[19c]
(Ernest Markham died in 1937. Author)

'Défi'
From Lemoine.[18]

'Dianthiflora Rubra Plena'
F. Morel. 1900.[18]

'Earl of Beaconsfield'
(Cripps & Son) – A free-flowering kind, having brilliant purple, well-formed blossoms of a striking and highly ornamental character.[10b]
Of the Viticella type, with very deep brownish-purple flowers, for which a Certificate was granted.[9b]
Rich purple.[1]

'Edouard André'
Product of a cross between *C.* 'Francois Morel' and viticella 'Kermesina' and dedicated to M. Edouard André, Editor-in-Chief of *Revue Horticole*. By M. F. Morel. Four tepals. Violet.[25k]
By Morel.[28a]

'Elegans'
(Lemoine). Reddy violet with red bands.[6]

'Erecta'[6]
Compared with viticella 'Nana'. Up to 40cms in height. Solitary blue flowers.[25c]

'Étincelle'
Red.[25l]

'FÉLIX FAURE'[27]
Lilac.

'FRANCOFURTENSIS'
C. francofurtensis, Rinz. - One of the earlier Continental hybrid varieties of the Viticella type, its parents being *C. patens* and *C. viticella coerulea*. The leaves resemble those of *C. viticella*. The flowers are of moderate size and of a deep purplish-blue colour, but it is now superseded.[23b]
'Francofurtensis'. 4 tepals. Purple. Blooms July-Nov.[16a]
Purple blue. 4-6 tepals.[24]
Deep purplish blue. Same as Guascoi.[28a]

'FRANÇOIS MOREL'
Flowers of a violet red, with a bar on each sepal of bright velvety red.[9c]
'Star of India' x *C. viticella rubro-grandiflora*. Morel.[19a]

'GEORG OHNET'
Lemoine. Light violet.[28a]

'GLADSTONE'
Blue.[27]
Jan Kleef. Boskoop. 1897.[18]

'GRANDIFLORA ROSEA'
From M. Alfroy, Lieusaint, Paris. 1849.[18]

'GREY LADY'
E Markham.[19d]

'GRINGOIRE'
(Lemoine 1895). Lilac blue. Semi-double.[28a]

'GUASCOI'
C.guascoi, Guasco (*Horticole Belgique*, vii, t.37; *L'Illustration Horticole*, iv.,t.117) – A hybrid variety, obtained between *C. viticella* and *C. patens*. The foliage resembles that of the former plant, while the flowers are moderate-sized, and of a deep purplish-violet colour. It is now superseded.[23c]

'HENRY CHAPLIN'
Carmine.[22]

'HORTULANUS WILKE'[27]
Pink.

'HORTULANUS WITTE'[27]
Blue.

'INTERMEDIA'

C. intermedia, Bonamy – This variety was discovered in the nursery of MM. Bonamy frères, of Toulouse, in 1866, as a chance seedling, in a bed near to where *C. integrifolia* and *C. viticella coerula*, its supposed parents, were growing. The leaves resemble those of *C. viticella*, being often pinnatisect, with variously-formed leaflets, while the flowers are bell-shaped, of moderate size, and of a blue colour. MM. Bonamy state that since they first found *C. intermedia*, they have made several sowings of its seeds, the results of which have convinced them that it really came from *C. viticella* and *C. integrifolia*, since the seedlings have often reverted to the two parents, as well as yielded singular variations.[23d]

'INTERMEDIA ROSEA'

C. intermedia 'Rosea', Bonamy – An erect-growing, ornamental, sub-shrubby clematis which, though attaining about six or seven feet in height, is not of climbing habit. The leaves are variable in form, but approach those of *C. Viticella*, being often pinnatisect, with the ovate-oblong leaflets decurrent behind. It is a free-blooming plant, with bell-shaped horizontal or nodding flowers, large as compared with those of most of the non-climbing species, of a pleasing lilac-rose colour, the sepals being broad and mucronate. The flowers altogether bear much resemblance in form to those of the Viticella group, and are developed effectively above the foliage branching panicles of eight of ten together; so abundant indeed are these in the adult plants, that they have the appearance of a huge bouquet. The plant is suitable for low walls or trellises, or for furnishing the naked trunks of trees occupying prominent positions. The variety is a seedling from *C. intermedia*, which was itself a chance seedling in the nurseries of MM. Bonamy, of Toulouse.[23d]

'IRIS'

Lemoine. Reddish -Violet.[6, 28a]

'JULIETTE DODU'[18]

'KAISER WILHELM'[27]

Blue.

'KONINGIN WILHELMINA'[27]

Blue.

'KSIAZE ALBERT'[27]

'LA FRAICHEUR'

C. No. 137 (pale rose) x *C. Viticella alba*. As strong growing as Viticella, but with large flowers. Morel.[19a]

'LADY BOVILL'

Jackman (*Floral Magazine*, t. 370; *Revue Horticole* (1876), 190, with tab.) – This variety of the Viticella type is quite dissimilar to all others which have been obtained, in the cupped form of its blossoms. The plant is of vigorous growth, and

has ternate leaves, with broad cordate downy leaflets. The flowers consist of from four to six sepals, which are downy externally, very broad, concave, and overlapping so as to form a cup-shaped flower, about four inches across. The colour of the sepals is a clear soft greyish-blue, or what is now called pure mauve, the stamens being of a light-brown tint, with pale-coloured filaments. The flower-buds are reflexed and remarkably downy, and the plant is a free and continuous bloomer.[23e]
Grey-blue. Cup shaped.[16a]
Hybrid with lanuginosa. Jackman 1867.[24]
Jackman (C. Lady Bovill, Hort). Fls. cup-formed, sepals being concave and little or not at all recurved at the ends; fls. 4in across; sepals 4-6, greyish blue; stamens light brown. Moore & Jackman.[2] Greyish-blue.[28a] (See Plate 115, page 168.)

'LADY GRAY'
From Ernest Markham [19d]

'LAMARTINE'
(Lemoine 1895). Pale blue. Double.[28a]

'LA MAUVE'
C. 'La Mauve', Cobbett – A variety of the Viticella type, of free-flowering habit. The leaves are ternate, with ovate leaflets. The flowers are of a light mauve colour, shaded with violet, and of good substance.[23f]
Cobbett. Light mauve.[28a]

'LA NANCEINNE'
La Nancéienne (Lemoine 1890). Dark violet. Double.[6, 28a]

'LANUGINOSA PALLIDA'
(Messrs Jackman & Son, Woking) – This variety, like those exhibited last year, by the same growers, was raised from *C. lanuginosa*, crossed with some of the best forms of the *Viticella* family. The present, like those just alluded to, had flat expanded flowers, and was very distinct in colour, being lilac, with reddish bars down the centre of the sepals. It will form a pretty contrast with the darker kinds. Second-class certificate.[13]

'LA POURPRE'
Lemoine.[18]

'LEONIDAS'[6]
Similar to 'Kermesina' but larger.[28a]
Purple flowers.[5]

'LILACINA FLORIBUNDA'
Cripps. One of this year's new kind. The colour is a pale grey-lilac, conspicuously veined in the petals; is an abundant bloomer.[10e]
Hort. (C. lilicina floribunda, Hort. C. floribunda, Hort.) Fls. pale grey-lilac, conspicuously veined. *Garden* 18.p.389 (note) – An abundant bloomer. Produced

in an English garden in 1880.[2]
Grey-lilac with darker veins.[26]

'LOUISE CARRIÈRE'

Carrière, E A. Clématite Louise Carrière. [25g]
(*Revue Horticole* January 1880, p.10, with a coloured plate) – A very elegant variety, intermediate between C.Viticella and C. Viticella venosa. It has the habit of the former, associated with purple-lilac veined flowers about 2in in diameter. The sepals are usually five or six in number, rarely four, traversed by a broad paler band down the centre, and suddenly recurved at the apex. M. Carrière describes this variety as a valuable acquisition, valuable on account of its hardiness, the beauty of its flowers associated with graceful foliage, and for the long duration of its flowering season, which last year extended to the end of November, in spite of the severe weather. Against a north-east wall its foliage and flowers were uninjured after frosts of 9°-14°.[10c]
'Louise Carrière' New. 6-7cm across. Brilliant Lilac rose. Veined.[16a]
Bluish-lilac with pale bar.[28a]

'MADAME FURTADO-HEINE'[6]

From M. Christen of Versailles. Red.[25j]
Christen. Vinous red.[28a]

'MADAME MOSER'

(Lemoine 1890). Yellowish-white.[28a]

'MAGNIFICA'

Very large and finely-formed flowers of a soft purple colour, each petal having a sharp bar of red down the centre, producing in the flower the appearance of a four or five rayed star.[12]
Carrière, E A. Clematis Viticella magnifica. From M. Paillet of Fontenay-aux-Roses.[25d]

'MAJOR'

C. Viticella 'Major'. Hort. – An improved form of the typical C. Viticella, and superseding it for garden purposes. It is a handsome, free-growing, moderately vigorous hardy climber, with pinnately-parted leaves, and four-sepaled, semi-expanded flowers, about two inches across, of a reddish plum-colour, with green stamens, produced freely and continuously from July to September.[23m]
Purple. Four tepals. Hort.[24]

'MARMORATA'

This pretty variety belongs to the Viticella group (see Plate 114, page 168), and has the habit of *C. viticella venosa*, flowering both profusely and successively. The leaves are pinnatisect, the basal pinnae being ternate. The flower-buds are dropping, and the flowers nearly the size of those of *C. v. venosa*, composed of four remarkably broad sepals, of a light mauve colour, marked with a three-ribbed bar, the whole surface of the flowers being speckled with white, in such a manner as to give it a veiny or marbled appearance. It is a very distinct and desirable variety. The sepals are

strongly recurved, which gives a distinct character to the flowers.[23g]
Lilac. Jackman.[24]
Jackman (*C. marmorata*.Hort). Fls. rather small with 4 broad sepals, greyish-blue, 3 longitudinal bars. Moore & Jackman J1,f.2; same plate in *Flore des Serres* 20,2008 (opp.p.17)[2]
Jackman. Light mauve, speckled white.[28a]

'MARQUIS DE DAMPIERRE'
(Lemoine). White. Carmine veins.[28a]

'MATHIEU DE DOMBASLE'
Small double. Violet-mauve.[28a]
Hybrid Viticella. Double flowers of violet-mauve, July-Sept.[30]

'MOAT STAR'
E. Markham.[19d]

'MODESTA'
C. modesta, Modeste-Guérin. One of the hybrids of the Viticella type, obtained between *C. lanuginosa* and *C. viticella*, and partaking of the free-growing and free-flowering character manifested by most of the varieties of this cross. The leaves are pinnatisect, with bold ovate leaflets. The flowers are comparatively large and expanded, of fine form, bright blue, veined with deeper blue along the centre of the sepals. It is rather a pretty plant, but now superseded.[23h]
'Modesta'. Blooms 8-9cms across. Lovely lilac-red in bright violet background. Strong plant.[16a]
C. Modesta, Modeste-Guérin (= C.v. x C.lanuginosa). Flowers well expanded, large, bright blue, bars deeper coloured.[2]
Of greater garden interest for their enhanced floral beauty are the hybrids of which *C. viticella* has been a parent. They include large-flowering forms such as Modesta.[30]
(Said to be the same plant as 'Prince Charles' and rediscovered in New Zealand. Author)

'MONSIEUR GRANDEAU'
Lemoine. Pale mauve with violet edges.[6, 28a]

'MONSIEUR TISSERAND'
Lemoine. White with bluish edges.[6, 28a]

'MOOREANA'
Another seedling, assuming more or less of the converging character of *viticella*. The flowers were larger than in Amethystina, and of a deep violet colour; the sepals very much recurved at the margins. Commendation.[13]
Very closely resembling *C. viticella* in the form of the flowers; colour deep violet.[12]
Jackman – One of a batch of seedlings raised between *C. lanuginosa* and *C. viticella*, but partaking of the general character of the latter parent. The flowers are large for this type, with erect sepals, much recurved at the edge, and forming a

convergent flower, of a deep violet colour. It has not been sent out.[23m]
Florida x *Viticella*.[21b]
Dark violet. Jackman 1864.[24]
(Jackman), deep violet. Not introduced?[28b]

'MRS JAMES BATEMAN'

C. 'Mrs James Bateman'. Jackman – A variety of the Viticella group, and a free and successional bloomer, not producing the profuse continuous mass of flowers characteristic of the Jackmanii type, but nevertheless continuing to yield throughout the season an abundant crop of its showy blossoms. It originated from some of the seedlings of the Jackmanii group once more crossed with *C. lanuginosa*, and produces bold ternate leaves, with large broad cordate acuminate leaflets, the blossom-buds being erect and woolly. The flowers have, for the most part, six sepals, and when they first open are of a deep reddish plum-colour, passing to lavender or mauve as the flowers become older, the red of the bar fading out less quickly; the tuft of stamens is conspicuous, the anthers being slightly tinted with reddish lilac. The illustration gives a good idea of the character of the flowers.[23i]
6 tepals. Lovely lavender blue. Flowers July-Oct.[16a]
Violet purple. Cripps. Hybrid Viticella Venosa.[24] (See also Plate 113, page 167.)

'MULTIFLORA RUBRA PLENA'

Morel.1900.[18]

'NANA'

Clematis viticella 'Nana'. E. A. Carrière.[25a]
Clematis viticella 'Nana'. E. A. Carrière.[25b]
One of the novelties of the French gardens is a *Clematis viticella* 'Nana', which was raised at the Paris Museum. Its flowers resemble those of the species, but are larger, and of a rosy lilac. The plant is only from 16-20ins high, and is not very floriferous, but perpetual-blooming. In fact, its shoots as they are developed are terminated by flowers, in such a manner that the plant is almost constantly provided with them. This is dwarf and not climbing, and its flowers are brought forth in succession during the summer.[9a]
C. viticella 'Nana'. Carrière. A remarkable dwarf variety, raised at the Jardin du Muséum in Paris, and differing from the type in not being of climbing habit, but producing short erect stems, and forming a compact bush of 1-2ft high, which becomes covered with continuous masses of flowers of a rosy-lilac colour, larger than those of the type, but corresponding with them in form. It is a remarkable variety, and shows how greatly the habit of a plant may be modified without the loss of specific identity.[23a]
The most distinct in habit is var. nana which grows little more than 1 yard high, and is rather a bush than a climber. It was raised in Paris by M. Carrière.[3]
Rose-purple, and only 3ft tall. The species is often used as a stock for grafting on the large-flowered hybrids, especially on the continent, but the practice is not commendable, as it increases the risk of die-back or wilt disease.[30]
A dwarf form described by Carrière in 1869.[4]
(We may speculate that this plant was a cross between a viticella and an integrifolia. Author.)

'NÉGRESSE'
Lemoine. Dark velvety-purple.[28a]

'NEIGE ET CERISE'
White edged. Cherry red.[28a]

'NIGRICANS'
C. 'Nigricans', Simon-Louis – A Continental variety apparently of the Viticella section. The leaves are not described. The flowers are of moderate size, four-sepaled, of a very deep purple colour, shaded almost to black.[23j]
4 tepals. Dark purple, dark stamens.[16a]

'N. VAN KLEEF'[27]
Violet.

'OLGAE'[27]
Blue.[27]
Cross of *C. integrifolia* and *C. viticella*. Named after Russian botanist Olga Fedtshenko.[17]

'ORIFLAMME'
Red flower.[25m]
C .F. Morel x *C. Viticella Kermesina*. The markings of the sepals of the seed parent have been preserved but on a much more vivid ground colour.[19a]
Small, violet-red with flecks of white.[28a]

'OTHELLO'
Othello, Cripps. This belongs to the Viticella section, being a seedling from *C. viticella venosa*. The leaves are ternate, with ovate leaflets. The flowers are six-sepaled, the sepals of a deep violet-purple, and the filaments of the anthers green. It is very much in the way of *C. rubella*, on which it is no improvement.[23j]
Othello. The flowers which are of a rich deep purple colour, about 4in across, though earlier in the season they are said to be fully double this size.[10d]
Othello, Cripps. Has flowers of medium size of a deep velvety-purple. Being one of the viticella type, it is a free flowerer, and continues to bear till late in autumn.[10e]
Otello - purple.[25m]
Othello, Cripps (= *C.* var. rubra x *C. Flammula*). Fls. of medium size, of a deep velvety purple; continues blooming until October.[10d]
Cripps. Lilac purple.[6, 28a]

'PALLIDA'
Jackman – A cross-bred variety between *C. lanuginosa* and *C. Viticella*. The flowers are large, broad-petalled, and expanded, lilac, with reddish bars down the sepals. It is, however, so far inferior to the varieties of the Jackmanii type, that it has been discarded.[25a]
(Jackman), lilac with red bars.[28a]

'PALMYRE'
Lemoine. White with carmine edges.[28a]

'PELLIERI'

A cross between *C. viticella* with a *C. lanuginosa*.[25h]

'POURPRE MAT' (Dull purple)

A.M. Sept 10, 1935. From Mr E. Markham. Commencing to flower at a time when many clematis of its type are past their best, this plant is a specially useful one. It is a vigorous grower and attains a height of 18ft. The flowers are 5in in diameter and of an attractive purple colour. The late William Robinson introduced it from France.[19b] Deep purple violet.[28a]

The last of all the large-flowered clematis to bloom, and, for that reason alone, must be regarded as a precious plant. Beginning to bloom at the end of August, the vigorous growth is soon lost beneath its canopy of rich, glowing crimson-purple flowers, which sweep in graceful folds to the ground. This handsome kind will develop 18 feet of growth in one season.[19c]

Of greater interest for their enhanced floral beauty are the hybrids of which *C. viticella* has been a parent. They include large-flowering forms such as 'Pourpre Mat'.[30]

'PROPHÉTESSE'[18]

'PURPUREA-HYBRIDA'

C. 'Purpurea-Hybrida', Modeste-Guérin. This variety belongs to the Viticella section, and in habit and foliage resembles the hybrids of the Jackmanii type. Less rich and velvety than in *C. Jackmanii*, having red veins running through the sepals; they are freely produced, and successional, but the variety is now superseded.[23k]

Modeste-Guérin (= C.V. x C. Jackmanii). Fls 4-6in across, deep purple violet, with red veins, but not barred.[2]

Modeste-Guérin. Deep purplish-violet.[28a]

'PUVIS DE CHAVANNES'

Lemoine. Dark purple.[28a]

'RETICULATA'

Violet.[16a]

'ROSEA'

Small, rose.[28b]

'RUBENS'

(Lemoine). Bluish purple.[6, 28a]

'RUBRA'

The old red-flowered form of the species, known to Philip Miller, and so named by Weston in 1774, when it was on sale in London nurseries. Whether the *C. viticella rubra* of present-day gardens is the same clone is not known.[5]

'RUBRA GRANDIFLORA' [8, 7, 25i, 29]

C. viticella 'Rubra Grandiflora'. Jackman – This is one of the most beautiful of the

Viticella forms. The leaves are pinnately-divided, or sometimes biternate, the leaflets being sometimes entire and ovate, sometimes divided into the three segments. The flowers, which are abundant and successional, measure about three inches across, and are composed of from four to six sepals of a rich bright claret-crimson, with green stamens. This charming variety has much the habit of *C. viticella venosa*, and like it is a most valuable acquisition. The profusion of blossoms and the distinctness of colour – it and C. 'Madame Grange' being the nearest approaches to a crimson clematis yet obtained – render it exceedingly effective.[23n] It is the variety *par excellence* that can lay claim to be a red-flowered clematis. The blooms are not large, but they are produced with remarkable freedom, and it is also a continuous bloomer. It possesses a singularly robust habit, and it is, therefore, well adapted for planting in shaded, moist situations, and where it may be too cold or too wet for the more delicate forms to do well.[10a]
From M. Louis Paillet, horticulteur à Châtenay, près Sceaux (Seine).[25i]
Red. 4-5 tepals. Jackman 1870.[24]
Flower has brilliant red flush.[6]
Purplish carmine. Medium size.[28a] (See also Plate 113, page 168.)

'SIDONIE'[28a]

'SIRENE'[18]

'STELLA'
E Markham.[19d]

'STOLEN KISS'
E Markham.[19d]

'THEMIS'
Lemoine. Carmine red.[28a]

'THOMAS MOORE'
Clematis Viticella var. amethystina & Mooreana.[15]
C. 'Thomas Moore', Jackman (*Florist and Pomologist*, 1869, 265,with tab) – this is one of the finest hybrids of the Viticella type, the flowers being of a bold and well-contrasted character, and the plants of a vigorous habit. The leaves are large and pinnatisect, with ovate leaflets, which are much acuminate. The flowers consist of from four to six long narrowish sepals, and are very large, amongst the largest indeed of the purple-flowered sorts, being often as much as from eight to nine inches across, of a deep rich brownish-violet, and having a very prominent tuft of white stamens, which gives to them something of the appearance of giant passion-flowers. The buds are long, dull dark purple, and deflexed, and the sepals, when extended, are more elliptic than ovate. The flowers are produced in successional and copious masses. The fine contrast between the sepals and the stamens entitles it to take a prominent place amongst the ornamental varieties of modern times.[23l]
Thomas Moore. New. 6-9 petals. Violet red. Flowers July-Oct.[16a]
Large violet-red flower.[25l]
Flower is 14-16cms wide. Violet- red.[6]

'VAGABONE'
Morel. 1900.[18]

'VENOSA'
Clematis viticella 'Venosa'. Hort.[14, 7b, 20, 25e, 16b]
This beautiful clematis is said to have been raised about 1855, either by M. Krampen, of Rosskothen, in Germany, or by M. Wilke, of Arnhem, in the Netherlands, the reputed parents being *Clematis patens* and *Atragene alpina* – a somewhat doubtful origin. It is of free growth and moderate vigour, the stems being slender and branching, and the leaves pinnately parted, the leaflets, especially the lower pair, being ternate. The flower-buds are erect, of a brownish-purple, and expand into full round handsome flowers, measuring from four to five inches across, and composed of five or six roundish ovate sepals; the colour is a pleasing tint of reddish-purple, paler towards the base of the sepals, in the centre of each of which is a five-ribbed bar more distinctly tinted with red, the entire surface being elegantly veined with crimson; while the central tuft of stamens, with white filaments and dark purple anthers, stands out in bold relief. It is remarkably free, bearing a long succession of flowers, and is, even now, one of the most ornamental of the many kinds in cultivation.[231]
Florida x Viticella.[21a]
Violet purple. Lemoine.[24]
Very vigorous.[251]
Reddish-purple.[28a]

'VENOSA GRANDIFLORA'[16b]
6-7 tepals, hyb. vitic. Venosa. Lemoine.[24]
Lemoine.[28a]

'VIVIAND MOREL'
Viviand-Morel. Product of a cross between viticella 'Rosa' and viticella 'Kermesina' and dedicated to M. Viviand-Morel, Chief of a Lyons nursery. From M.F. Morel. 6 tepals. Red.[25k]
(Morel).[28a]

'WILLIAM ELLIOT'[27]
Blue.

References

1. *American Gardening* (1898) p.390.
   André, Edouard *see Revue Horticole*.
2. Bailey, L.H. (1900) *Standard Cyclopaedia of Horticulture*, p.332.
3. Bean, W.J. (1877) *The Garden*.
4. Bean, W.J. (1939) *Trees and Shrubs Hardy in the British Isles*, p.664.
5. Bean, W.J. (1939) *Wall Shrubs and Hardy Climbers*, Paris, pp.71-72.
6. Boucher, G. & Mottet, S. (1898) *Les Clematides*. Paris, pp.71-72.
   Carrière, E.A. see *Gardener's Chronicle & Revue Horticole.*.
   Davis, K.C. *see The Garden*.
7. a) Gand, O. (1874) *Flores des Serres et des Jardins de l'Europe*, p.2052.
   b) Houtte, Louis van (1858) ditto, XIII, p.137. t.1364.
8. *Florist* (1872) p.350.

9. a) *Florist & Pomologist* (1872) p.144.
   b)   Ditto   (1878) p.111.
   c)   Ditto   (1878) p.168.
   d)   Ditto   (1886) p.168.
10. a) *The Garden* (May 1878) p.486.
   b)   Ditto   (June 1878) p.611.
   c)   Ditto   (Feb. 1880) p.136.
   d)   Ditto   (Sept. 1880) p.228.
   e)   Ditto   (Oct. 1880) p.389.
   f)   Ditto   (Aug. 1894) p.115.
   g   Ditto   (1896) p.131.
   h) Davis, K.C. Ditto *1899) ix c.
11. *Gardener's Chronicle* (1879) p.683. (E.A. Carrière).
12. *Gardener's Magazine* (1867) x. 134.
13. *Gardener's Weekly Magazine & Floricultural Cabinet* (1864) p.383.
14. Henderson, *Illustrated Bouquet* II, t.30.
15. Horticultural Society of London (1864) *Proceedings IV.* p.159.
16. *Illustrierte Monatshefte* (1884) Stuttgart, p.141.
         Ditto   Ditto   p.142.
17. Johnson, Magnus (1987) *Clematis International* 4. 13.
18. Johnson, Magnus (1997) *The Genus Clematis*, Södertälje.
19. a) *Journal of the Royal Horticultural Society* (1900) XXIV, 31.
   b)   Ditto   (1935) LX, 511.
   c)   Ditto   (1936) LXI, 344 & clxxiv.
   d)   Ditto   (1937) LXII, 160.
20. Krampen, Wilhelm (1861) *Wochenschrift IV*, 232.
21. a) Kuntze, O. (1885) *Botanischen Vereins der Prinvz Brandenburg*, p.185.
   b)   Ditto   Ditto   p.187.
22. Markham, Ernest (1935) *Clematis*, p.117.
23. a) Moore, T. & Jackman, G. (1877) *The Clematis as a Garden Flower*, p.81.
   b)   Ditto   Ditto   p.89.
   c)   Ditto   Ditto   p.91.
   d)   Ditto   Ditto   p.93.
   e)   Ditto   Ditto   p.96.
   f)   Ditto   Ditto   p.97.
   g)   Ditto   Ditto   p.105.
   h)   Ditto   Ditto   p.106.
   i)   Ditto   Ditto   p.108.
   j)   Ditto   Ditto   p.110.
   k)   Ditto   Ditto   p.113.
   l)   Ditto   Ditto   p.119.
   m)   Ditto   Ditto   p.123.
   n)   Ditto   Ditto   p.124.
      National Horticultural Magazine see Spingarn, J.E.
24. *Practische Beschrijvende Lijst* (1890) Boksoop.
25. a) *Revue Horticole* (1869) p.307.
   b)   Ditto   (1872) p.60.
   c)   Ditto   (1874) p.400.
   d)   Ditto   (1876) p.110.
   e) Carrière, E.A. Ditto (1878) p.279.
   f)   Ditto   Ditto (1879) p.350.
   g) *Revue Horticole* (1880) pp.10-11.
   h)   Ditto   (1880) p.227.
   i)   Ditto   (1887) p.341.
   j) Carrière, E.A. Ditto (1889) p.108.
   k) *Revue Horticole* (1889) p.371.
   l) André, E. Ditto (1893) p.204.
   m) Ditto   Ditto (1893) p.206.
26a. Robinson, W. (1912) *The Virgin's Bower*, John Murray, London.
26b. Schrek, R.M., *Personal Communication*, 1996.
27. Snoeijer, W. (1991) *Clematis Index*, Boksoop.
28. a) Spingarn, J.E. (1935) *National Horticulture Magazine* 14, 64.
   b) Ditto   Ditto   14, 935.
29. Stapf, O. (1930) *Index Londinensis II*. p.236.
30. Whitehead, S./r. (1959) *Clematis* p.165.

INDEX

Page numbers in **bold** refer to illustrations

Also by John Howells
THE ROSE AND THE CLEMATIS – As Good Companions,

The companion volume to
TROUBLE FREE CLEMATIS – The Viticellas.

In this title, the author, John Howells, a former Chairman of the British Clematis Society, introduces his readers to the idea of growing roses and clematis together so that the natural beauty of each plant is enhanced and dramatised by its companion. He points out that the climbing rose is the natural companion of the clematis and when the two are grown together, the overall effect can be dramatic. To help his readers achieve the desired effect, the author sets out, with the aid of clear, easy-to-follow illustrated instructions, the precise course of action to be followed.

Written in plain, straightforward language, John Howells covers every possible aspect of the subject. As well as details of classification, in which he suggests the best plants for the job, he also provides important seasonal growing information including autumn and spring pruning techniques, planting details and invaluable advice on the use of colour. The vexed question of diseases and pests is also dealt with at length.

THE ROSE AND THE CLEMATIS - As Good Companions, written by an author with a deep practical knowledge and love of his subject, is a useful guide to the growing of clematis in a novel and effective way. The reader is shown what can be achieved and will derive much inspiration from the numerous colour photographs which feature so prominently throughout this attractive book. It is a fitting companion to the current title which takes the subject of clematis growing a stage further.

206 pages, 140 colour plates, 75 colour & black and white drawings.
11 x 8½in/279 x 216mm   ISBN 1 870673 19 0   **£19.95**.